The *Honest Mom* Journal

THE STRUGGLING MOM'S GUIDE TO STRUGGLING LESS

Libby Ward

Disclaimer: My story is a personal account of my own journey with motherhood and sometimes my mental health struggles like depression and should not be taken as a substitute for professional advice. I strongly believe that anyone who feels they may need support should seek the help of a qualified health care professional – they were vital in my own journey, and are trained to find the right support for each person's unique and individual care. If you are in crisis – know there are many compassionate and expert teams available to help you. Call 911 or consult with your local emergency department.
If you need help you deserve it, and can get it.

First paperback edition October 2022

ISBN 978-1-5011-7321-9

diaryofanhonestmom.com

FOREWORD

Libby Ward
Content Creator | Public Speaker | Writer
⊙ ♪ @diaryofanhonestmom
⊕ diaryofanhonestmom.com

Have you ever laid in bed at night replaying all the ways you didn't show up as the mom you wanted to be that day?

Do you struggle with mom guilt?

Do you ever feel like you are not enough for all the expectations there are of you as a mother?

Do you have negative self-talk?

Do you ever catch yourself comparing yourself to other moms and wishing or wondering why you aren't more like them?

Motherhood is hard and it's even harder when we feel like we are alone. For a long time I struggled with things like overwhelm, guilt, comparison, over-stimulation, mental health, lack of support, being the default parent, burnout, loss of identity and so much more. I became resentful, exhausted and it negatively affected my whole experience of motherhood. I was trying to be everything to everyone and I couldn't be.

Something had to change.

Self-awareness was my path to change.

Now I share about these things and more to help moms know they are not alone and inspire them to change that by getting honest about their circumstances, practicing self-compassion and prioritizing themselves.

If you are holding this journal in your hands you have already taken the most important step. Awareness is key. You are acknowledging that something has to change, whether that be your mindset or your actions. The fact that you are aware and trying, is evidence that you already are a good mom.

Taking the time to fill out this journal every morning and night is going to help you to re-frame your thoughts and expectations so you can go to bed at night proud of the mom you are and confident about what you are choosing to prioritize because the reality is that we can't do it all.

I genuinely hope that after finishing this journal you can look back on your days, weeks and months and see just how good you are actually doing: especially given the circumstances you are in.

—

We're done with comparison, with shame, with guilt and with not feeling like we're enough.

I know motherhood is hard, but you can do hard things.

You already are, and I am so proud of you.

Libby

THE HONEST MOM JOURNAL GUIDE

So how does it work?
For those who are familiar with my content on *Instagram* and *Tiktok* and *my blog*, this journal will probably be easier to follow than if you have no context at all so feel free to go binge my content: **@diaryofanhonestmom, www.diaryofanhonestmom.com.**

This guide is meant to give you the information you need in order to get the most out of the exercise.

Here are the basics:
Set aside 5-10 quiet (as quiet as you can get) minutes each morning & night to fill it out honestly. In the morning you'll be setting the tone and setting realistic expectations for the day, and in the evening you'll be focusing on all the positives from the day and giving yourself grace for the things that didn't go as you had hoped.

With those things in mind, lets go over some basic definitions:

Expectations: *a strong belief that something will happen or be the case in the future*

Sometimes we don't consciously recognize when we have expectations until they become unmet (aka that your baby would sleep through the night by the time they were 6 months old or that you would have the time to organize the closets today). Part of checking our expectations is getting real about what you hope or think might happen and then taking the time to consider what might make it a reality or not and what you can do to adjust the expectation.

Capacity: the *maximum amount that something can contain.*

This is the amount of mental and physical energy you have along with your current knowledge, mental health and overall ability to do the things you want or need to do. Everything from our health, to the number of responsibilities we have, to our partner status, to the amount of sleep we are getting, to the support system we do or don't have and more, affect our capacity. If we don't acknowledge what our capacity is and how it can change, our ability to set realistic expectations or give ourselves grace when things don't go to plan is extremely limited.

Grace: permission to forgive your mistakes, lapses in judgment, and hurtful behaviour, because no one is perfect

It's the idea that you can look back on your imperfections or the ways you didn't measure up to your own values, standards or expectations and accept that you are enough and valuable anyway. We need to give ourselves grace everyday because the reality is that we are imperfect humans. Giving ourselves grace takes the energy we put into GUILT and releases it, so we can get back thoughts and actions that are joyful, restful or productive.

ONTO THE GOODS...

MORNiNG

Get Affirmed: Read it out loud even if it feels silly. Set the tone for your day.

Get Aware: We all have resources, abilities or circumstances that can support us as moms and we all have things that make momming a bit harder. The weather, our finances, a visit from a friend, being healthy, access to therapy or any number of big or small things can get us through a day. And the opposite: Parenting solo, struggling financially, being sick, mental health, trauma, lack of sleep, a rainy day, a stressful life event and more can make it harder. Write these things down so you know where to turn or so you can give yourself grace when it gets hard.

Get Your Priorities Straight: It's hard to remember in the moment but we can't have or do it all: especially in motherhood. Maybe we can't be equal amounts of these things everyday but going into the day knowing that being peaceful, present or productive is the goal will help you to let go of the "I should be..." feelings when you are cleaning, playing, resting etc. This is meant to help you practise away those "I should" feelings.

Get Going: A to do list, but realistic. It sucks to get to the end of the day and not cross much off. The idea of this is the *must do's* are the only things that are really important and will have negative consequences if they are not done: AKA: feeding the kids or going to an important appointment. Nice to do's are those things you want to get done like the laundry or getting outside but won't have big consequences if you don't do them. Get to do's are just a way to look at how lucky we are to do some things like snuggling your baby or being in a safe loving home.

Get Real: A place to write down anything else you are feeling about as the day gets going. It's important to get real about everything that's going on so we're not surprised by feelings that come up later in the day or mis-labelling our feelings as a result of something they *aren't* a result of. For example: I might write down that I am sleep deprived and haven't had a break in weeks. So when I am triggered by my kids being noisy in my face, I can remember it has more to do with how I am feeling than *them* being the main source of my feelings and I can come up with a plan without guilt: like putting the TV on.

EVENiNG

The purpose of the evening reflection is to frame your day realistically and with grace rather than guilt.

Get Reflective: Find something you are proud of and realize that it's quite an accomplishment considering what obstacles you faced. So maybe you are proud of yourself for working out even though you were feeling tired. Or maybe you are proud of yourself for remaining calm while your child had a meltdown *even though* you wanted to react angrily. This is a reflection of your own actions and choices even though you were struggling with something. Not a place to say "I am proud that I didn't xyz even though he/she was being unreasonable". It's about "me and I" statements. This is the self awareness piece.

Get Some Grace: Guilt can sometimes be productive, like when it alerts us to our behaviours or actions that don't align with our value system and makes us aware of opportunities for change or growth. Guilt can also be very unproductive, where we feel bad for something either out of our control or for something we shouldn't feel guilty for: like getting time alone or going to work or cleaning the house instead of playing.

Get Positive: For something you accomplished, pick some things from your get going list or other things you did to remind yourself you DID do something today. It's too easy to feel like we didn't do anything. A mental win is something you thought or realized through your day that you have been working on like choosing to let go of the pressure to get everything done. It could be giving yourself grace for something or recognizing a trigger before you let it out, etc.

Get Reminiscent: A place to look back on your day with kind eyes. Remember the hilarious thing your kid said or the way your baby smiled at you. Remember an encouraging thing a friend said to you. It's easy to look back on our day with judgemental eyes. Practice looking back with kindness and grace. Write down something that brought you joy that is so simple but could be easily forgotten.

PROGRESS NOT PERFECTION

And finally:
I hope this guide helps you to find joy, peace and goodness in your day. I hope that by getting aware of your circumstances, obstacles and supports, you can set realistic expectations and be proud of the good mom you are. We are not meant to be perfect. They say that moms who question if they are good moms, usually are the ones who are. The fact that you are reading this means you are aware of yourself and therefore are a good mom.

It is about *progress* not *perfection*.

An honest mom is a good mom. I'm proud of you for taking the time to get honest so you can see that you are a good mom and find joy in this crazy, hard and beautiful journey.

I'm not here to tell you how to be a good mom, you already are one.

You just need to see it.

LET'S GET INTO IT...

Date: _____

Get Affirmed:

I'm a good mom because I love my kid(s) and I am aware enough to know I can't do it all. Every family, every struggle and every season of my motherhood is different and so I won't let one day define what kind of mom I am. My expectations should change with my reality. *I am trying and that matters.*

Get Aware: *Because our unique situation impacts our capacity and knowing this can change our whole day.*

A reality that could make today easier: _____

_____

A reality that could make today harder: _____

_____

Get Your Priorities Straight *You can't be everything all day everyday. Today, what are you going to prioritize? (Choose one).*

peaceful   *present*   *productive*

Get Going: *A realistic to do list: may include anything from appointments to surviving the day.*

Must do	Nice to do	Get to do
important	want	gratitude

Get Real:

Get as honest as possible about what you are feeling, what you need, what capacity you have to give and what makes the most sense for your family today. How can you use awareness to adjust your expectations to your current lived reality? How are you going to be a good mom without striving for perfection? You've got this!

_____

_____

_____

Get Reflective :

EVENING

I am proud of myself for:

even though:

Get Some Grace:

I am feeling guilty for:

and so I need to:
(Choose one)

Give myself grace and try again tomorrow

Give myself grace and apologize

Give myself grace and seek out tools to improve

I don't need grace, this guilt is not necessary or productive

Get Positive: *You did it! What did you get done today? This is your "tada" list. Fed the kids? Made an appointment? The possibilities are endless.*

Something you accomplished:

A mental win:

Get Reminiscent:

It's so easy to end our day thinking about what we didn't do or how we messed up. It's easy to forget the special little moments that made us laugh or felt meaningful, too. What's a small thing that you'd like to remember from today?

I can't do it all everyday, but everyday I do something that matters. I'm not defined by what I do but rather who I am. I am a human who loves her kids and I deserve as much grace as anyone else. I deserve to be cared for, too. I am a good mom, and I know this because *I am here, I am aware* and *I am trying.*

Date: _____

Get Affirmed:

I'm a good mom because I love my kid(s) and I am aware enough to know I can't do it all. Every family, every struggle and every season of my motherhood is different and so I won't let one day define what kind of mom I am. My expectations should change with my reality. *I am trying and that matters.*

Get Aware: *Because our unique situation impacts our capacity and knowing this can change our whole day.*

A reality that could make today easier: _____

_____

A reality that could make today harder: _____

_____

Get Your Priorities Straight   *You can't be everything all day everyday. Today, what are you going to prioritize? (Choose one).*

peaceful   present   productive

Get Going: *A realistic to do list: may include anything from appointments to surviving the day.*

Must do important	**Nice to do** want	**Get to do** gratitude

Get Real:

Get as honest as possible about what you are feeling, what you need, what capacity you have to give and what makes the most sense for your family today. How can you use awareness to adjust your expectations to your current lived reality? How are you going to be a good mom without striving for perfection? You've got this!

_____

_____

_____

Get Reflective :

I am proud of myself for:

_____

_____

_____

even though: _____

_____

Get Some Grace:

I am feeling guilty for: _____

_____

and so
I need to:
(Choose one)

- Give myself grace and try again tomorrow
- Give myself grace and apologize
- Give myself grace and seek out tools to improve
- I don't need grace, this guilt is not necessary or productive

Get Positive:

You did it! What did you get done today? This is your "tada" list.
Fed the kids? Made an appointment? The possibilities are endless.

Something you accomplished: _____

A mental win: _____

Get Reminiscent:

It's so easy to end our day thinking about what we didn't do or how we messed up. It's easy to forget the special little moments that made us laugh or felt meaningful, too. What's a small thing that you'd like to remember from today?

_____

_____

_____

I can't do it all everyday, but everyday I do something that matters. I'm not defined by what I do but rather who I am. I am a human who loves her kids and I deserve as much grace as anyone else. I deserve to be cared for, too. I am a good mom, and I know this because *I am here, I am aware* and *I am trying.*

Get Affirmed:

I'm a good mom because I love my kid(s) and I am aware enough to know I can't do it all. Every family, every struggle and every season of my motherhood is different and so I won't let one day define what kind of mom I am. My expectations should change with my reality. *I am trying and that matters.*

Get Aware: *Because our unique situation impacts our capacity and knowing this can change our whole day.*

A reality that could make today easier: _____

_____

A reality that could make today harder: _____

_____

Get Your Priorities Straight *You can't be everything all day everyday. Today, what are you going to prioritize? (Choose one).*

peaceful   present   productive

Get Going: *A realistic to do list: may include anything from appointments to surviving the day.*

Must do	**Nice to do**	**Get to do**
important	want	gratitude

Get Real:

Get as honest as possible about what you are feeling, what you need, what capacity you have to give and what makes the most sense for your family today. How can you use awareness to adjust your expectations to your current lived reality? How are you going to be a good mom without striving for perfection? You've got this!

_____

_____

_____

EVENING

Get Reflective :

I am proud of myself for:

even though:

Get Some Grace:

I am feeling guilty for:

and so I need to:
(Choose one)

- Give myself grace and try again tomorrow
- Give myself grace and apologize
- Give myself grace and seek out tools to improve
- I don't need grace, this guilt is not necessary or productive

Get Positive:

You did it! What did you get done today? This is your "tada" list. Fed the kids? Made an appointment? The possibilities are endless.

Something you accomplished:

A mental win:

Get Reminiscent:

It's so easy to end our day thinking about what we didn't do or how we messed up. It's easy to forget the special little moments that made us laugh or felt meaningful, too. What's a small thing that you'd like to remember from today?

I can't do it all everyday, but everyday I do something that matters. I'm not defined by what I do but rather who I am. I am a human who loves her kids and I deserve as much grace as anyone else. I deserve to be cared for, too. I am a good mom, and I know this because *I am here, I am aware* and *I am trying.*

Get Affirmed:

I'm a good mom because I love my kid(s) and I am aware enough to know I can't do it all. Every family, every struggle and every season of my motherhood is different and so I won't let one day define what kind of mom I am. My expectations should change with my reality. *I am trying and that matters.*

Get Aware: *Because our unique situation impacts our capacity and knowing this can change our whole day.*

A reality that could make today easier: _____

_____

A reality that could make today harder: _____

_____

Get Your Priorities Straight *You can't be everything all day everyday. Today, what are you going to prioritize? (Choose one).*

peaceful   present   productive

Get Going: *A realistic to do list: may include anything from appointments to surviving the day.*

| **Must do** | **Nice to do** | **Get to do** |
important	want	gratitude

Get Real:

Get as honest as possible about what you are feeling, what you need, what capacity you have to give and what makes the most sense for your family today. How can you use awareness to adjust your expectations to your current lived reality? How are you going to be a good mom without striving for perfection? You've got this!

_____

_____

_____

Get Reflective :

I am proud of myself for:

even though:

Get Some Grace:

I am feeling guilty for:

and so
I need to:
(Choose one)

Give myself grace and try again tomorrow

Give myself grace and apologize

Give myself grace and seek out tools to improve

I don't need grace, this guilt is not necessary or productive

Get Positive: *You did it! What did you get done today? This is your "tada" list. Fed the kids? Made an appointment? The possibilities are endless.*

Something you accomplished:

A mental win:

Get Reminiscent:

It's so easy to end our day thinking about what we didn't do or how we messed up. It's easy to forget the special little moments that made us laugh or felt meaningful, too. What's a small thing that you'd like to remember from today?

I can't do it all everyday, but everyday I do something that matters. I'm not defined by what I do but rather who I am. I am a human who loves her kids and I deserve as much grace as anyone else. I deserve to be cared for, too. I am a good mom, and I know this because *I am here, I am aware* and *I am trying.*

Date: _____

MORNING

Get Affirmed:

I'm a good mom because I love my kid(s) and I am aware enough to know I can't do it all. Every family, every struggle and every season of my motherhood is different and so I won't let one day define what kind of mom I am. My expectations should change with my reality. *I am trying and that matters.*

Get Aware: *Because our unique situation impacts our capacity and knowing this can change our whole day.*

A reality that could make today easier: _____

_____

A reality that could make today harder: _____

_____

Get Your Priorities Straight *You can't be everything all day everyday. Today, what are you going to prioritize? (Choose one).*

peaceful   *present*   *productive*

Get Going: *A realistic to do list: may include anything from appointments to surviving the day.*

Must do	Nice to do	Get to do
important	want	gratitude
_____	_____	_____
_____	_____	_____
_____	_____	_____

Get Real:

Get as honest as possible about what you are feeling, what you need, what capacity you have to give and what makes the most sense for your family today. How can you use awareness to adjust your expectations to your current lived reality? How are you going to be a good mom without striving for perfection? You've got this!

_____

_____

_____

Get Reflective :

I am proud of myself for:

even though:

Get Some Grace:

I am feeling guilty for:

*and so
I need to:*
(Choose one)

Give myself grace and try again tomorrow

Give myself grace and apologize

Give myself grace and seek out tools to improve

I don't need grace, this guilt is not necessary or productive

Get Positive:
*You did it! What did you get done today? This is your "tada" list.
Fed the kids? Made an appointment? The possibilities are endless.*

Something you accomplished:

A mental win:

Get Reminiscent:

It's so easy to end our day thinking about what we didn't do or how we messed up. It's easy to forget the special little moments that made us laugh or felt meaningful, too. What's a small thing that you'd like to remember from today?

I can't do it all everyday, but everyday I do something that matters. I'm not defined by what I do but rather who I am. I am a human who loves her kids and I deserve as much grace as anyone else. I deserve to be cared for, too. I am a good mom, and I know this because *I am here, I am aware* and *I am trying.*

Date: _____

Get Affirmed:

I'm a good mom because I love my kid(s) and I am aware enough to know I can't do it all. Every family, every struggle and every season of my motherhood is different and so I won't let one day define what kind of mom I am. My expectations should change with my reality. *I am trying and that matters.*

Get Aware: *Because our unique situation impacts our capacity and knowing this can change our whole day.*

A reality that could make today easier: _____

_____

A reality that could make today harder: _____

_____

Get Your Priorities Straight *You can't be everything all day everyday. Today, what are you going to prioritize? (Choose one).*

peaceful   present   productive

Get Going: *A realistic to do list: may include anything from appointments to surviving the day.*

Must do	Nice to do	Get to do
important	want	gratitude
_____	_____	_____
_____	_____	_____
_____	_____	_____

Get Real:

Get as honest as possible about what you are feeling, what you need, what capacity you have to give and what makes the most sense for your family today. How can you use awareness to adjust your expectations to your current lived reality? How are you going to be a good mom without striving for perfection? You've got this!

_____

_____

_____

Get Reflective :

I am proud of myself for: _____

_____

even though: _____

_____

Get Some Grace:

I am feeling guilty for: _____

_____

and so
I *need* to:
(Choose one)

- Give myself grace and try again tomorrow
- Give myself grace and apologize
- Give myself grace and seek out tools to improve
- I don't need grace, this guilt is not necessary or productive

Get Positive:
You did it! What did you get done today? This is your "tada" list. Fed the kids? Made an appointment? The possibilities are endless.

Something you accomplished: _____

A mental win: _____

Get Reminiscent:

It's so easy to end our day thinking about what we didn't do or how we messed up. It's easy to forget the special little moments that made us laugh or felt meaningful, too. What's a small thing that you'd like to remember from today?

_____

_____

_____

I can't do it all everyday, but everyday I do something that matters. I'm not defined by what I do but rather who I am. I am a human who loves her kids and I deserve as much grace as anyone else. I deserve to be cared for, too. I am a good mom, and I know this because *I am here, I am aware* and *I am trying.*

Get Affirmed:

I'm a good mom because I love my kid(s) and I am aware enough to know I can't do it all. Every family, every struggle and every season of my motherhood is different and so I won't let one day define what kind of mom I am. My expectations should change with my reality. *I am trying and that matters.*

Get Aware: *Because our unique situation impacts our capacity and knowing this can change our whole day.*

A reality that could make today easier: _____

_____

A reality that could make today harder: _____

_____

Get Your Priorities Straight *You can't be everything all day everyday. Today, what are you going to prioritize? (Choose one).*

peaceful   present   productive

Get Going: *A realistic to do list: may include anything from appointments to surviving the day.*

Must do	**Nice to do**	**Get to do**
important	want	gratitude
_____	_____	_____
_____	_____	_____
_____	_____	_____

Get Real:

Get as honest as possible about what you are feeling, what you need, what capacity you have to give and what makes the most sense for your family today. How can you use awareness to adjust your expectations to your current lived reality? How are you going to be a good mom without striving for perfection? You've got this!

_____

_____

_____

Get Reflective :

I am proud of myself for: _____

_____

_____

even though: _____

_____

Get Some Grace:

I am feeling guilty for: _____

_____

*and so
I need to:*
(Choose one)

○ Give myself grace and try again tomorrow

○ Give myself grace and apologize

○ Give myself grace and seek out tools to improve

○ I don't need grace, this guilt is not necessary or productive

Get Positive: *You did it! What did you get done today? This is your "tada" list. Fed the kids? Made an appointment? The possibilities are endless.*

Something you accomplished: _____

A mental win: _____

Get Reminiscent:

It's so easy to end our day thinking about what we didn't do or how we messed up. It's easy to forget the special little moments that made us laugh or felt meaningful, too. What's a small thing that you'd like to remember from today?

_____

_____

_____

I can't do it all everyday, but everyday I do something that matters. I'm not defined by what I do but rather who I am. I am a human who loves her kids and I deserve as much grace as anyone else. I deserve to be cared for, too. I am a good mom, and I know this because *I am here, I am aware* and *I am trying.*

Date: _____

Get Affirmed:

I'm a good mom because I love my kid(s) and I am aware enough to know I can't do it all. Every family, every struggle and every season of my motherhood is different and so I won't let one day define what kind of mom I am. My expectations should change with my reality. *I am trying and that matters.*

Get Aware:

Because our unique situation impacts our capacity and knowing this can change our whole day.

A reality that could make today easier: _____

_____

A reality that could make today harder: _____

_____

Get Your Priorities Straight

You can't be everything all day everyday. Today, what are you going to prioritize? (Choose one).

peaceful   present   productive

Get Going:

A realistic to do list: may include anything from appointments to surviving the day.

Must do important	**Nice to do** want	**Get to do** gratitude
_____	_____	_____
_____	_____	_____
_____	_____	_____

Get Real:

Get as honest as possible about what you are feeling, what you need, what capacity you have to give and what makes the most sense for your family today. How can you use awareness to adjust your expectations to your current lived reality? How are you going to be a good mom without striving for perfection? You've got this!

_____

_____

_____

Get Reflective :

I am proud of myself for:

even though:

Get Some Grace:

I am feeling guilty for:

and so
I need to:
(Choose one)

Give myself grace and try again tomorrow

Give myself grace and apologize

Give myself grace and seek out tools to improve

I don't need grace, this guilt is not necessary or productive

Get Positive:
You did it! What did you get done today? This is your "tada" list. Fed the kids? Made an appointment? The possibilities are endless.

Something you accomplished:

A mental win:

Get Reminiscent:

It's so easy to end our day thinking about what we didn't do or how we messed up. It's easy to forget the special little moments that made us laugh or felt meaningful, too. What's a small thing that you'd like to remember from today?

I can't do it all everyday, but everyday I do something that matters. I'm not defined by what I do but rather who I am. I am a human who loves her kids and I deserve as much grace as anyone else. I deserve to be cared for, too. I am a good mom, and I know this because *I am here, I am aware* and *I am trying.*

Get Affirmed:

I'm a good mom because I love my kid(s) and I am aware enough to know I can't do it all. Every family, every struggle and every season of my motherhood is different and so I won't let one day define what kind of mom I am. My expectations should change with my reality. *I am trying and that matters.*

Get Aware: *Because our unique situation impacts our capacity and knowing this can change our whole day.*

A reality that could make today easier: _____

_____

A reality that could make today harder: _____

_____

Get Your Priorities Straight *You can't be everything all day everyday. Today, what are you going to prioritize? (Choose one).*

peaceful   present   productive

Get Going: *A realistic to do list: may include anything from appointments to surviving the day.*

Must do important	Nice to do want	Get to do gratitude

Get Real:

Get as honest as possible about what you are feeling, what you need, what capacity you have to give and what makes the most sense for your family today. How can you use awareness to adjust your expectations to your current lived reality? How are you going to be a good mom without striving for perfection? You've got this!

_____

_____

_____

Get Reflective :

I am proud of myself for: _____

_____

_____

even though: _____

_____

Get Some Grace:

I am feeling guilty for: _____

_____

and so
I need to:
(Choose one)

    Give myself grace and try again tomorrow

    Give myself grace and apologize

    Give myself grace and seek out tools to improve

    I don't need grace, this guilt is not necessary or productive

Get Positive:
You did it! What did you get done today? This is your "tada" list. Fed the kids? Made an appointment? The possibilities are endless.

Something you accomplished: _____

A mental win: _____

Get Reminiscent:

It's so easy to end our day thinking about what we didn't do or how we messed up. It's easy to forget the special little moments that made us laugh or felt meaningful, too. What's a small thing that you'd like to remember from today?

_____

_____

_____

I can't do it all everyday, but everyday I do something that matters. I'm not defined by what I do but rather who I am. I am a human who loves her kids and I deserve as much grace as anyone else. I deserve to be cared for, too. I am a good mom, and I know this because *I am here, I am aware* and *I am trying.*

Get Affirmed:

I'm a good mom because I love my kid(s) and I am aware enough to know I can't do it all. Every family, every struggle and every season of my motherhood is different and so I won't let one day define what kind of mom I am. My expectations should change with my reality. *I am trying and that matters.*

Get Aware: *Because our unique situation impacts our capacity and knowing this can change our whole day.*

A reality that could make today easier: _____

_____

A reality that could make today harder: _____

_____

Get Your Priorities Straight *You can't be everything all day everyday. Today, what are you going to prioritize? (Choose one).*

peaceful   present   productive

Get Going: *A realistic to do list: may include anything from appointments to surviving the day.*

Must do	Nice to do	Get to do
important	want	gratitude
_____	_____	_____
_____	_____	_____
_____	_____	_____

Get Real:

Get as honest as possible about what you are feeling, what you need, what capacity you have to give and what makes the most sense for your family today. How can you use awareness to adjust your expectations to your current lived reality? How are you going to be a good mom without striving for perfection? You've got this!

_____

_____

_____

Get Reflective :

I am proud of myself for: _____

_____

even though: _____

Get Some Grace:

I am feeling guilty for: _____

and so
I need to:
(Choose one)

- Give myself grace and try again tomorrow
- Give myself grace and apologize
- Give myself grace and seek out tools to improve
- I don't need grace, this guilt is not necessary or productive

Get Positive: *You did it! What did you get done today? This is your "tada" list. Fed the kids? Made an appointment? The possibilities are endless.*

Something you accomplished: _____

A mental win: _____

Get Reminiscent:

It's so easy to end our day thinking about what we didn't do or how we messed up. It's easy to forget the special little moments that made us laugh or felt meaningful, too. What's a small thing that you'd like to remember from today?

_____

_____

_____

I can't do it all everyday, but everyday I do something that matters. I'm not defined by what I do but rather who I am. I am a human who loves her kids and I deserve as much grace as anyone else. I deserve to be cared for, too. I am a good mom, and I know this because *I am here, I am aware* and *I am trying.*

Date: _____

Get Affirmed:

I'm a good mom because I love my kid(s) and I am aware enough to know I can't do it all. Every family, every struggle and every season of my motherhood is different and so I won't let one day define what kind of mom I am. My expectations should change with my reality. *I am trying and that matters.*

Get Aware: *Because our unique situation impacts our capacity and knowing this can change our whole day.*

A reality that could make today easier: _____

_____

A reality that could make today harder: _____

_____

Get Your Priorities Straight   *You can't be everything all day everyday. Today, what are you going to prioritize? (Choose one).*

peaceful   *present*   *productive*

Get Going: *A realistic to do list: may include anything from appointments to surviving the day.*

Must do important	**Nice to do** want	**Get to do** gratitude

Get Real:

Get as honest as possible about what you are feeling, what you need, what capacity you have to give and what makes the most sense for your family today. How can you use awareness to adjust your expectations to your current lived reality? How are you going to be a good mom without striving for perfection? You've got this!

_____

_____

_____

Get Reflective :

I am proud of myself for: _____

_____

_____

even though: _____

_____

Get Some Grace:

I am feeling guilty for: _____

and so
I need to:
(Choose one)

- Give myself grace and try again tomorrow
- Give myself grace and apologize
- Give myself grace and seek out tools to improve
- I don't need grace, this guilt is not necessary or productive

Get Positive: *You did it! What did you get done today? This is your "tada" list. Fed the kids? Made an appointment? The possibilities are endless.*

Something you accomplished: _____

A mental win: _____

Get Reminiscent:

It's so easy to end our day thinking about what we didn't do or how we messed up. It's easy to forget the special little moments that made us laugh or felt meaningful, too. What's a small thing that you'd like to remember from today?

_____

_____

_____

I can't do it all everyday, but everyday I do something that matters. I'm not defined by what I do but rather who I am. I am a human who loves her kids and I deserve as much grace as anyone else. I deserve to be cared for, too. I am a good mom, and I know this because *I am here, I am aware* and *I am trying.*

Get Affirmed:

I'm a good mom because I love my kid(s) and I am aware enough to know I can't do it all. Every family, every struggle and every season of my motherhood is different and so I won't let one day define what kind of mom I am. My expectations should change with my reality. *I am trying and that matters.*

Get Aware: *Because our unique situation impacts our capacity and knowing this can change our whole day.*

A reality that could make today easier: _____

_____

A reality that could make today harder: _____

_____

Get Your Priorities Straight *You can't be everything all day everyday. Today, what are you going to prioritize? (Choose one).*

peaceful   present   productive

Get Going: *A realistic to do list: may include anything from appointments to surviving the day.*

Must do	**Nice to do**	**Get to do**
important	want	gratitude
_____	_____	_____
_____	_____	_____
_____	_____	_____

Get Real:

Get as honest as possible about what you are feeling, what you need, what capacity you have to give and what makes the most sense for your family today. How can you use awareness to adjust your expectations to your current lived reality? How are you going to be a good mom without striving for perfection? You've got this!

_____

_____

_____

Get Reflective :

I am proud of myself for: _____

_____

_____

even though: _____

_____

Get Some Grace:

I am feeling guilty for: _____

_____

*and so
I need to:*
(Choose one)

- Give myself grace and try again tomorrow
- Give myself grace and apologize
- Give myself grace and seek out tools to improve
- I don't need grace, this guilt is not necessary or productive

Get Positive:

You did it! What did you get done today? This is your "tada" list. Fed the kids? Made an appointment? The possibilities are endless.

Something you accomplished: _____

A mental win: _____

Get Reminiscent:

It's so easy to end our day thinking about what we didn't do or how we messed up. It's easy to forget the special little moments that made us laugh or felt meaningful, too. What's a small thing that you'd like to remember from today?

_____

_____

_____

I can't do it all everyday, but everyday I do something that matters. I'm not defined by what I do but rather who I am. I am a human who loves her kids and I deserve as much grace as anyone else. I deserve to be cared for, too. I am a good mom, and I know this because *I am here, I am aware* and *I am trying.*

Get Affirmed:

I'm a good mom because I love my kid(s) and I am aware enough to know I can't do it all. Every family, every struggle and every season of my motherhood is different and so I won't let one day define what kind of mom I am. My expectations should change with my reality. *I am trying and that matters.*

Get Aware: *Because our unique situation impacts our capacity and knowing this can change our whole day.*

A reality that could make today easier: _____

_____

A reality that could make today harder: _____

_____

Get Your Priorities Straight *You can't be everything all day everyday. Today, what are you going to prioritize? (Choose one).*

peaceful   *present*   *productive*

Get Going: *A realistic to do list: may include anything from appointments to surviving the day.*

Must do important	Nice to do want	Get to do gratitude

Get Real:

Get as honest as possible about what you are feeling, what you need, what capacity you have to give and what makes the most sense for your family today. How can you use awareness to adjust your expectations to your current lived reality? How are you going to be a good mom without striving for perfection? You've got this!

_____

_____

_____

Get Reflective :

I am proud of myself for: _____

_____

_____

even though: _____

_____

Get Some Grace:

I am feeling guilty for: _____

_____

*and so
I need to:*
(Choose one)

☐ Give myself grace and try again tomorrow

☐ Give myself grace and apologize

☐ Give myself grace and seek out tools to improve

☐ I don't need grace, this guilt is not necessary or productive

Get Positive:

You did it! What did you get done today? This is your "tada" list. Fed the kids? Made an appointment? The possibilities are endless.

Something you accomplished: _____

A mental win: _____

Get Reminiscent:

It's so easy to end our day thinking about what we didn't do or how we messed up. It's easy to forget the special little moments that made us laugh or felt meaningful, too. What's a small thing that you'd like to remember from today?

_____

_____

_____

I can't do it all everyday, but everyday I do something that matters. I'm not defined by what I do but rather who I am. I am a human who loves her kids and I deserve as much grace as anyone else. I deserve to be cared for, too. I am a good mom, and I know this because *I am here, I am aware* and *I am trying.*

Date: _____

Get Affirmed:

I'm a good mom because I love my kid(s) and I am aware enough to know I can't do it all. Every family, every struggle and every season of my motherhood is different and so I won't let one day define what kind of mom I am. My expectations should change with my reality. *I am trying and that matters.*

Get Aware: *Because our unique situation impacts our capacity and knowing this can change our whole day.*

A reality that could make today easier: _____

_____

A reality that could make today harder: _____

_____

Get Your Priorities Straight *You can't be everything all day everyday. Today, what are you going to prioritize? (Choose one).*

peaceful   present   productive

Get Going: *A realistic to do list: may include anything from appointments to surviving the day.*

Must do	**Nice to do**	**Get to do**
important	want	gratitude

Get Real:

Get as honest as possible about what you are feeling, what you need, what capacity you have to give and what makes the most sense for your family today. How can you use awareness to adjust your expectations to your current lived reality? How are you going to be a good mom without striving for perfection? You've got this!

_____

_____

_____

Get Reflective :

EVENING

I am proud of myself for:

even though:

Get Some Grace:

I am feeling guilty for:

and so
I need to:
(Choose one)

   Give myself grace and try again tomorrow

   Give myself grace and apologize

   Give myself grace and seek out tools to improve

   I don't need grace, this guilt is not necessary or productive

Get Positive: *You did it! What did you get done today? This is your "tada" list. Fed the kids? Made an appointment? The possibilities are endless.*

Something you accomplished:

A mental win:

Get Reminiscent:

It's so easy to end our day thinking about what we didn't do or how we messed up. It's easy to forget the special little moments that made us laugh or felt meaningful, too. What's a small thing that you'd like to remember from today?

I can't do it all everyday, but everyday I do something that matters. I'm not defined by what I do but rather who I am. I am a human who loves her kids and I deserve as much grace as anyone else. I deserve to be cared for, too. I am a good mom, and I know this because *I am here, I am aware* and *I am trying.*

TiME TO REFLECT

This part is *really* important.

It's where you pay attention to the hard work you have put into this week in real life and also in these journal pages. It is the checkpoint that you stop at to look at the state of your sense of self of self-worth, self-awareness, self-acceptance and the state of your expectations.

When you do this, keep in mind it is about **progress** not perfection. It is about getting honest about yourself, your motherhood and your circumstances so that you can see what your capacity truly is. Then use this knowledge to have more grace for yourself, less guilt and eventually, more confidence in the things you intentionally choose to prioritize [which are based on your values & capacity].

Slowly but surely, you'll create more space for you again and that space will allow you to enjoy motherhood more, and struggle less. Let's do it.

—

You Are Worthy
You are a human being with human needs, even if you are a mom. You are worthy of love, of care, of rest, of play, of sleep, of nourishment, of joy and of grace. Being imperfect is a part of being human and acknowledging that you have needs is essential to making changes that help those needs get met.

Do you believe you are worthy of these things? ☐ Yes ☐ No ☐ Sometimes

In what ways have you started to see your perception of yourself change this week?

When have you actively chosen **you** this week? What did you do? How did it feel?

In what ways would you like to see your mindset towards yourself change more?

—

You Have Awareness
Your circumstances are unique, I hope that this week you have been able to become more aware of them and be radically honest about: what resources and supports you have at your disposal; what roadblocks you are facing when it comes to meeting your own expectations; and what values drive how your prioritize that time, energy and overall capacity that you have at this stage of life.

What parts of your life (finances, support system, partner status, mental health or physical health limitations, child stages/ages abilities, personal capacity and day to day circumstances etc) have you become more aware of this week?

How has this awareness helped you to fight guilt, give yourself grace, utilize some of your support system or change expectations for yourself?

How can you become even more self aware this week? How can you use this awareness to struggle a little less with your day to day reality or the way you feel?

—

You Accept Yourself
You cannot be all the things to all the people all the time. You have certain values, limitations and priorities. With the knowledge that you are worthy and the awareness of your reality, you can begin to accept that you cannot prioritize everything all the time. With the nature of being human and life being busy, your capacity will change and with that you can accept yourself.
What are you learning to accept about the limitations you might have that impact your motherhood journey?

What things do you still struggle to accept that you can't do? Or what things are you struggling to accept that you can't change?

What are you going to do differently this coming week that will help you to be more accepting of what you can't change or are struggling to change?

—

Your Expectations are Changing
You have expectations. We all do. We are told that it's important to change them. But how? And which ones? And for how long? The only way we can find the time to prioritize our own wellness and struggle less in motherhood is by letting some things go–even if it's just for a season or a day! By focusing on your priorities, values, limitations and supports I hope you have been able to realize what things you can lower expectations on or take off the priority list all together.

What was your biggest priority this week, and do you think it was a realistic priority to have?

What expectations were you able to shift based on the self-awareness you have been practicing?

What expectations would you like to see yourself shift even more?

Have you been feeling guilt or shame about changing expectations? How can you work on your self-worth & grace in order to combat the negative feelings that come with letting some things go?

Great job. You are doing the work. You are taking the time from the million other things you have to do and using it to be intentional about your motherhood journey and your experience of it. It is not easy. But it is worth it and I am so proud of you. Here's to another week of Honest Mothering. You've got this.

Date: _____

Get Affirmed:

I'm a good mom because I love my kid(s) and I am aware enough to know I can't do it all. Every family, every struggle and every season of my motherhood is different and so I won't let one day define what kind of mom I am. My expectations should change with my reality. *I am trying and that matters.*

Get Aware: *Because our unique situation impacts our capacity and knowing this can change our whole day.*

A reality that could make today easier: _____

_____

A reality that could make today harder: _____

_____

Get Your Priorities Straight   *You can't be everything all day everyday. Today, what are you going to prioritize? (Choose one).*

peaceful   present   productive

Get Going: *A realistic to do list: may include anything from appointments to surviving the day.*

Must do	Nice to do	Get to do
important	want	gratitude
_____	_____	_____
_____	_____	_____
_____	_____	_____

Get Real:

Get as honest as possible about what you are feeling, what you need, what capacity you have to give and what makes the most sense for your family today. How can you use awareness to adjust your expectations to your current lived reality? How are you going to be a good mom without striving for perfection? You've got this!

_____

_____

_____

Get Reflective :

I am proud of myself for:

_____

_____

even though:

_____

Get Some Grace:

I am feeling guilty for:

_____

*and so
I need to:*
(Choose one)

- Give myself grace and try again tomorrow
- Give myself grace and apologize
- Give myself grace and seek out tools to improve
- I don't need grace, this guilt is not necessary or productive

Get Positive:

*You did it! What did you get done today? This is your "tada" list.
Fed the kids? Made an appointment? The possibilities are endless.*

Something you accomplished: _____

A mental win: _____

Get Reminiscent:

It's so easy to end our day thinking about what we didn't do or how we messed up. It's easy to forget the special little moments that made us laugh or felt meaningful, too. What's a small thing that you'd like to remember from today?

_____

_____

_____

I can't do it all everyday, but everyday I do something that matters. I'm not defined by what I do but rather who I am. I am a human who loves her kids and I deserve as much grace as anyone else. I deserve to be cared for, too. I am a good mom, and I know this because *I am here, I am aware* and *I am trying.*

Date: _____

Get Affirmed:

I'm a good mom because I love my kid(s) and I am aware enough to know I can't do it all. Every family, every struggle and every season of my motherhood is different and so I won't let one day define what kind of mom I am. My expectations should change with my reality. *I am trying and that matters.*

Get Aware: *Because our unique situation impacts our capacity and knowing this can change our whole day.*

A reality that could make today easier: _____

_____

A reality that could make today harder: _____

_____

Get Your Priorities Straight   *You can't be everything all day everyday. Today, what are you going to prioritize? (Choose one).*

peaceful   present   productive

Get Going: *A realistic to do list: may include anything from appointments to surviving the day.*

Must do	Nice to do	Get to do
important	want	gratitude

Get Real:

Get as honest as possible about what you are feeling, what you need, what capacity you have to give and what makes the most sense for your family today. How can you use awareness to adjust your expectations to your current lived reality? How are you going to be a good mom without striving for perfection? You've got this!

_____

_____

_____

Get Reflective :

I am proud of myself for: _____

_____

even though: _____

Get Some Grace:

I am feeling guilty for: _____

and so I need to:
(Choose one)

- Give myself grace and try again tomorrow
- Give myself grace and apologize
- Give myself grace and seek out tools to improve
- I don't need grace, this guilt is not necessary or productive

Get Positive: *You did it! What did you get done today? This is your "tada" list. Fed the kids? Made an appointment? The possibilities are endless.*

Something you accomplished: _____

A mental win: _____

Get Reminiscent:

It's so easy to end our day thinking about what we didn't do or how we messed up. It's easy to forget the special little moments that made us laugh or felt meaningful, too. What's a small thing that you'd like to remember from today?

_____

_____

I can't do it all everyday, but everyday I do something that matters. I'm not defined by what I do but rather who I am. I am a human who loves her kids and I deserve as much grace as anyone else. I deserve to be cared for, too. I am a good mom, and I know this because *I am here, I am aware* and *I am trying.*

Date: _____

Get Affirmed:

I'm a good mom because I love my kid(s) and I am aware enough to know I can't do it all. Every family, every struggle and every season of my motherhood is different and so I won't let one day define what kind of mom I am. My expectations should change with my reality. *I am trying and that matters.*

Get Aware:
Because our unique situation impacts our capacity and knowing this can change our whole day.

A reality that could make today easier: _____

_____

A reality that could make today harder: _____

_____

Get Your Priorities Straight
You can't be everything all day everyday. Today, what are you going to prioritize? (Choose one).

peaceful   present   productive

Get Going:
A realistic to do list: may include anything from appointments to surviving the day.

Must do	Nice to do	Get to do
important	want	gratitude

Get Real:

Get as honest as possible about what you are feeling, what you need, what capacity you have to give and what makes the most sense for your family today. How can you use awareness to adjust your expectations to your current lived reality? How are you going to be a good mom without striving for perfection? You've got this!

_____

_____

_____

Get Reflective :

I am proud of myself for:

_____

_____

_____

even though: _____

_____

Get Some Grace:

I am feeling guilty for: _____

_____

and so
I need to:
(Choose one)

- Give myself grace and try again tomorrow
- Give myself grace and apologize
- Give myself grace and seek out tools to improve
- I don't need grace, this guilt is not necessary or productive

Get Positive:

You did it! What did you get done today? This is your "tada" list.
Fed the kids? Made an appointment? The possibilities are endless.

Something you accomplished: _____

A mental win: _____

Get Reminiscent:

It's so easy to end our day thinking about what we didn't do or how we messed up. It's easy to forget the special little moments that made us laugh or felt meaningful, too. What's a small thing that you'd like to remember from today?

_____

_____

_____

I can't do it all everyday, but everyday I do something that matters. I'm not defined by what I do but rather who I am. I am a human who loves her kids and I deserve as much grace as anyone else. I deserve to be cared for, too. I am a good mom, and I know this because *I am here, I am aware* and *I am trying.*

Date: _____

Get Affirmed:

I'm a good mom because I love my kid(s) and I am aware enough to know I can't do it all. Every family, every struggle and every season of my motherhood is different and so I won't let one day define what kind of mom I am. My expectations should change with my reality. *I am trying and that matters.*

Get Aware:
Because our unique situation impacts our capacity and knowing this can change our whole day.

A reality that could make today easier: _____

_____

A reality that could make today harder: _____

_____

Get Your Priorities Straight
You can't be everything all day everyday. Today, what are you going to prioritize? (Choose one).

peaceful   present   productive

Get Going:
A realistic to do list: may include anything from appointments to surviving the day.

Must do	Nice to do	Get to do
important	want	gratitude

Get Real:

Get as honest as possible about what you are feeling, what you need, what capacity you have to give and what makes the most sense for your family today. How can you use awareness to adjust your expectations to your current lived reality? How are you going to be a good mom without striving for perfection? You've got this!

_____

_____

_____

Get Reflective :

I am proud of myself for: _____

_____

_____

even though: _____

_____

Get Some Grace:

I am feeling guilty for: _____

_____

and so
I need to:
(Choose one)

Give myself grace and try again tomorrow

Give myself grace and apologize

Give myself grace and seek out tools to improve

I don't need grace, this guilt is not necessary or productive

Get Positive:
You did it! What did you get done today? This is your "tada" list.
Fed the kids? Made an appointment? The possibilities are endless.

Something you accomplished: _____

A mental win: _____

Get Reminiscent:

It's so easy to end our day thinking about what we didn't do or how we messed up. It's easy to forget the special little moments that made us laugh or felt meaningful, too. What's a small thing that you'd like to remember from today?

_____

_____

_____

I can't do it all everyday, but everyday I do something that matters. I'm not defined by what I do but rather who I am. I am a human who loves her kids and I deserve as much grace as anyone else. I deserve to be cared for, too. I am a good mom, and I know this because *I am here, I am aware* and *I am trying.*

Date: _____

Get Affirmed:

I'm a good mom because I love my kid(s) and I am aware enough to know I can't do it all. Every family, every struggle and every season of my motherhood is different and so I won't let one day define what kind of mom I am. My expectations should change with my reality. *I am trying and that matters.*

Get Aware: *Because our unique situation impacts our capacity and knowing this can change our whole day.*

A reality that could make today easier: _____

_____

A reality that could make today harder: _____

_____

Get Your Priorities Straight *You can't be everything all day everyday. Today, what are you going to prioritize? (Choose one).*

peaceful   present   productive

Get Going: *A realistic to do list: may include anything from appointments to surviving the day.*

Must do	**Nice to do**	**Get to do**
important	want	gratitude

Get Real:

Get as honest as possible about what you are feeling, what you need, what capacity you have to give and what makes the most sense for your family today. How can you use awareness to adjust your expectations to your current lived reality? How are you going to be a good mom without striving for perfection? You've got this!

_____

_____

_____

Get Reflective :

I am proud of myself for:

even though:

Get Some Grace:

I am feeling guilty for:

and so
I need to:
(Choose one)

- Give myself grace and try again tomorrow
- Give myself grace and apologize
- Give myself grace and seek out tools to improve
- I don't need grace, this guilt is not necessary or productive

Get Positive:
You did it! What did you get done today? This is your "tada" list. Fed the kids? Made an appointment? The possibilities are endless.

Something you accomplished:

A mental win:

Get Reminiscent:

It's so easy to end our day thinking about what we didn't do or how we messed up. It's easy to forget the special little moments that made us laugh or felt meaningful, too. What's a small thing that you'd like to remember from today?

I can't do it all everyday, but everyday I do something that matters. I'm not defined by what I do but rather who I am. I am a human who loves her kids and I deserve as much grace as anyone else. I deserve to be cared for, too. I am a good mom, and I know this because *I am here, I am aware* and *I am trying.*

Get Affirmed:

I'm a good mom because I love my kid(s) and I am aware enough to know I can't do it all. Every family, every struggle and every season of my motherhood is different and so I won't let one day define what kind of mom I am. My expectations should change with my reality. *I am trying and that matters.*

Get Aware: *Because our unique situation impacts our capacity and knowing this can change our whole day.*

A reality that could make today easier: _____

_____

A reality that could make today harder: _____

_____

Get Your Priorities Straight *You can't be everything all day everyday. Today, what are you going to prioritize? (Choose one).*

peaceful   present   productive

Get Going: *A realistic to do list: may include anything from appointments to surviving the day.*

Must do	Nice to do	Get to do
important	want	gratitude

Get Real:

Get as honest as possible about what you are feeling, what you need, what capacity you have to give and what makes the most sense for your family today. How can you use awareness to adjust your expectations to your current lived reality? How are you going to be a good mom without striving for perfection? You've got this!

_____

_____

_____

Get Reflective :

I am proud of myself for: _____

_____

_____

even though: _____

_____

Get Some Grace:

I am feeling guilty for: _____

_____

and so
I need to:
(Choose one)

   Give myself grace and try again tomorrow

   Give myself grace and apologize

   Give myself grace and seek out tools to improve

   I don't need grace, this guilt is not necessary or productive

Get Positive:
You did it! What did you get done today? This is your "tada" list. Fed the kids? Made an appointment? The possibilities are endless.

Something you accomplished: _____

A mental win: _____

Get Reminiscent:

It's so easy to end our day thinking about what we didn't do or how we messed up. It's easy to forget the special little moments that made us laugh or felt meaningful, too. What's a small thing that you'd like to remember from today?

_____

_____

_____

I can't do it all everyday, but everyday I do something that matters. I'm not defined by what I do but rather who I am. I am a human who loves her kids and I deserve as much grace as anyone else. I deserve to be cared for, too. I am a good mom, and I know this because *I am here, I am aware* and *I am trying.*

Get Affirmed:

I'm a good mom because I love my kid(s) and I am aware enough to know I can't do it all. Every family, every struggle and every season of my motherhood is different and so I won't let one day define what kind of mom I am. My expectations should change with my reality. *I am trying and that matters.*

Get Aware: *Because our unique situation impacts our capacity and knowing this can change our whole day.*

A reality that could make today easier: _____

_____

A reality that could make today harder: _____

_____

Get Your Priorities Straight *You can't be everything all day everyday. Today, what are you going to prioritize? (Choose one).*

peaceful   present   productive

Get Going: *A realistic to do list: may include anything from appointments to surviving the day.*

Must do	**Nice to do**	**Get to do**
important	want	gratitude

Get Real:

Get as honest as possible about what you are feeling, what you need, what capacity you have to give and what makes the most sense for your family today. How can you use awareness to adjust your expectations to your current lived reality? How are you going to be a good mom without striving for perfection? You've got this!

_____

_____

_____

Get Reflective :

I am proud of myself for:

even though:

Get Some Grace:

I am feeling guilty for:

and so
I need to:
(Choose one)

- Give myself grace and try again tomorrow
- Give myself grace and apologize
- Give myself grace and seek out tools to improve
- I don't need grace, this guilt is not necessary or productive

Get Positive:

You did it! What did you get done today? This is your "tada" list. Fed the kids? Made an appointment? The possibilities are endless.

Something you accomplished:

A mental win:

Get Reminiscent:

It's so easy to end our day thinking about what we didn't do or how we messed up. It's easy to forget the special little moments that made us laugh or felt meaningful, too. What's a small thing that you'd like to remember from today?

I can't do it all everyday, but everyday I do something that matters. I'm not defined by what I do but rather who I am. I am a human who loves her kids and I deserve as much grace as anyone else. I deserve to be cared for, too. I am a good mom, and I know this because *I am here, I am aware* and *I am trying.*

Get Affirmed:

I'm a good mom because I love my kid(s) and I am aware enough to know I can't do it all. Every family, every struggle and every season of my motherhood is different and so I won't let one day define what kind of mom I am. My expectations should change with my reality. *I am trying and that matters.*

Get Aware: *Because our unique situation impacts our capacity and knowing this can change our whole day.*

A reality that could make today easier: _____

_____

A reality that could make today harder: _____

_____

Get Your Priorities Straight   *You can't be everything all day everyday. Today, what are you going to prioritize? (Choose one).*

peaceful   *present*   *productive*

Get Going: *A realistic to do list: may include anything from appointments to surviving the day.*

Must do	Nice to do	Get to do
important	want	gratitude

Get Real:

Get as honest as possible about what you are feeling, what you need, what capacity you have to give and what makes the most sense for your family today. How can you use awareness to adjust your expectations to your current lived reality? How are you going to be a good mom without striving for perfection? You've got this!

_____

_____

_____

Get Reflective :

I am proud of myself for:

_____

_____

_____

even though: _____

_____

Get Some Grace:

I am feeling guilty for: _____

_____

and so I need to:
(Choose one)

- Give myself grace and try again tomorrow
- Give myself grace and apologize
- Give myself grace and seek out tools to improve
- I don't need grace, this guilt is not necessary or productive

Get Positive:

You did it! What did you get done today? This is your "tada" list. Fed the kids? Made an appointment? The possibilities are endless.

Something you accomplished: _____

A mental win: _____

Get Reminiscent:

It's so easy to end our day thinking about what we didn't do or how we messed up. It's easy to forget the special little moments that made us laugh or felt meaningful, too. What's a small thing that you'd like to remember from today?

_____

_____

_____

I can't do it all everyday, but everyday I do something that matters. I'm not defined by what I do but rather who I am. I am a human who loves her kids and I deserve as much grace as anyone else. I deserve to be cared for, too. I am a good mom, and I know this because *I am here, I am aware* and *I am trying.*

Date: _____

Get Affirmed:

I'm a good mom because I love my kid(s) and I am aware enough to know I can't do it all. Every family, every struggle and every season of my motherhood is different and so I won't let one day define what kind of mom I am. My expectations should change with my reality. *I am trying and that matters.*

Get Aware: *Because our unique situation impacts our capacity and knowing this can change our whole day.*

A reality that could make today easier: _____

_____

A reality that could make today harder: _____

_____

Get Your Priorities Straight *You can't be everything all day everyday. Today, what are you going to prioritize? (Choose one).*

peaceful   *present*   *productive*

Get Going: *A realistic to do list: may include anything from appointments to surviving the day.*

Must do important	**Nice to do** want	**Get to do** gratitude

Get Real:

Get as honest as possible about what you are feeling, what you need, what capacity you have to give and what makes the most sense for your family today. How can you use awareness to adjust your expectations to your current lived reality? How are you going to be a good mom without striving for perfection? You've got this!

_____

_____

_____

Get Reflective :

I am proud of myself for:

even though:

Get Some Grace:

I am feeling guilty for:

and so
I need to:
(Choose one)

Give myself grace and try again tomorrow

Give myself grace and apologize

Give myself grace and seek out tools to improve

I don't need grace, this guilt is not necessary or productive

Get Positive:
You did it! What did you get done today? This is your "tada" list.
Fed the kids? Made an appointment? The possibilities are endless.

Something you accomplished:

A mental win:

Get Reminiscent:

It's so easy to end our day thinking about what we didn't do or how we messed up. It's easy to forget the special little moments that made us laugh or felt meaningful, too. What's a small thing that you'd like to remember from today?

I can't do it all everyday, but everyday I do something that matters. I'm not defined by what I do but rather who I am. I am a human who loves her kids and I deserve as much grace as anyone else. I deserve to be cared for, too. I am a good mom, and I know this because *I am here, I am aware* and *I am trying.*

Get Affirmed:

I'm a good mom because I love my kid(s) and I am aware enough to know I can't do it all. Every family, every struggle and every season of my motherhood is different and so I won't let one day define what kind of mom I am. My expectations should change with my reality. *I am trying and that matters.*

Get Aware:
Because our unique situation impacts our capacity and knowing this can change our whole day.

A reality that could make today easier: _____

_____

A reality that could make today harder: _____

_____

Get Your Priorities Straight
You can't be everything all day everyday. Today, what are you going to prioritize? (Choose one).

peaceful   present   productive

Get Going:
A realistic to do list: may include anything from appointments to surviving the day.

Must do	Nice to do	Get to do
important	want	gratitude
_____	_____	_____
_____	_____	_____
_____	_____	_____

Get Real:

Get as honest as possible about what you are feeling, what you need, what capacity you have to give and what makes the most sense for your family today. How can you use awareness to adjust your expectations to your current lived reality? How are you going to be a good mom without striving for perfection? You've got this!

_____

_____

_____

Get Reflective :

I am proud of myself for: _____

_____

_____

even though: _____

_____

Get Some Grace:

I am feeling guilty for: _____

and so
I need to:
(Choose one)

- Give myself grace and try again tomorrow
- Give myself grace and apologize
- Give myself grace and seek out tools to improve
- I don't need grace, this guilt is not necessary or productive

Get Positive:
You did it! What did you get done today? This is your "tada" list. Fed the kids? Made an appointment? The possibilities are endless.

Something you accomplished: _____

A mental win: _____

Get Reminiscent:

It's so easy to end our day thinking about what we didn't do or how we messed up. It's easy to forget the special little moments that made us laugh or felt meaningful, too. What's a small thing that you'd like to remember from today?

_____

_____

_____

I can't do it all everyday, but everyday I do something that matters. I'm not defined by what I do but rather who I am. I am a human who loves her kids and I deserve as much grace as anyone else. I deserve to be cared for, too. I am a good mom, and I know this because *I am here, I am aware* and *I am trying.*

Date: _____

Get Affirmed:

I'm a good mom because I love my kid(s) and I am aware enough to know I can't do it all. Every family, every struggle and every season of my motherhood is different and so I won't let one day define what kind of mom I am. My expectations should change with my reality. *I am trying and that matters.*

Get Aware: *Because our unique situation impacts our capacity and knowing this can change our whole day.*

A reality that could make today easier: _____

_____

A reality that could make today harder: _____

_____

Get Your Priorities Straight *You can't be everything all day everyday. Today, what are you going to prioritize? (Choose one).*

peaceful   present   productive

Get Going: *A realistic to do list: may include anything from appointments to surviving the day.*

Must do important	**Nice to do** want	**Get to do** gratitude
_____	_____	_____
_____	_____	_____
_____	_____	_____

Get Real:

Get as honest as possible about what you are feeling, what you need, what capacity you have to give and what makes the most sense for your family today. How can you use awareness to adjust your expectations to your current lived reality? How are you going to be a good mom without striving for perfection? You've got this!

_____

_____

_____

Get Reflective :

I am proud of myself for: _____

_____

_____

even though: _____

_____

Get Some Grace:

I am feeling guilty for: _____

_____

and so
I need to:
(Choose one)

- Give myself grace and try again tomorrow
- Give myself grace and apologize
- Give myself grace and seek out tools to improve
- I don't need grace, this guilt is not necessary or productive

Get Positive:

You did it! What did you get done today? This is your "tada" list. Fed the kids? Made an appointment? The possibilities are endless.

Something you accomplished: _____

A mental win: _____

Get Reminiscent:

It's so easy to end our day thinking about what we didn't do or how we messed up. It's easy to forget the special little moments that made us laugh or felt meaningful, too. What's a small thing that you'd like to remember from today?

_____

_____

_____

I can't do it all everyday, but everyday I do something that matters. I'm not defined by what I do but rather who I am. I am a human who loves her kids and I deserve as much grace as anyone else. I deserve to be cared for, too. I am a good mom, and I know this because *I am here, I am aware* and *I am trying.*

Date: _____

Get Affirmed:

I'm a good mom because I love my kid(s) and I am aware enough to know I can't do it all. Every family, every struggle and every season of my motherhood is different and so I won't let one day define what kind of mom I am. My expectations should change with my reality. *I am trying and that matters.*

Get Aware: *Because our unique situation impacts our capacity and knowing this can change our whole day.*

A reality that could make today easier: _____

_____

A reality that could make today harder: _____

_____

Get Your Priorities Straight *You can't be everything all day everyday. Today, what are you going to prioritize? (Choose one).*

peaceful   present   productive

Get Going: *A realistic to do list: may include anything from appointments to surviving the day.*

Must do	Nice to do	Get to do
important	want	gratitude
_____	_____	_____
_____	_____	_____
_____	_____	_____

Get Real:

Get as honest as possible about what you are feeling, what you need, what capacity you have to give and what makes the most sense for your family today. How can you use awareness to adjust your expectations to your current lived reality? How are you going to be a good mom without striving for perfection? You've got this!

_____

_____

_____

Get Reflective :

I am proud of myself for: _____

_____

even though: _____

_____

Get Some Grace:

I am feeling guilty for: _____

and so
I need to:
(Choose one)

    Give myself grace and try again tomorrow

    Give myself grace and apologize

    Give myself grace and seek out tools to improve

    I don't need grace, this guilt is not necessary or productive

Get Positive:
You did it! What did you get done today? This is your "tada" list. Fed the kids? Made an appointment? The possibilities are endless.

Something you accomplished: _____

A mental win: _____

Get Reminiscent:

It's so easy to end our day thinking about what we didn't do or how we messed up. It's easy to forget the special little moments that made us laugh or felt meaningful, too. What's a small thing that you'd like to remember from today?

_____

_____

I can't do it all everyday, but everyday I do something that matters. I'm not defined by what I do but rather who I am. I am a human who loves her kids and I deserve as much grace as anyone else. I deserve to be cared for, too. I am a good mom, and I know this because *I am here, I am aware* and *I am trying.*

Date: _____

MORNING

Get Affirmed:

I'm a good mom because I love my kid(s) and I am aware enough to know I can't do it all. Every family, every struggle and every season of my motherhood is different and so I won't let one day define what kind of mom I am. My expectations should change with my reality. *I am trying and that matters.*

Get Aware: *Because our unique situation impacts our capacity and knowing this can change our whole day.*

A reality that could make today easier: _____

_____

A reality that could make today harder: _____

_____

Get Your Priorities Straight *You can't be everything all day everyday. Today, what are you going to prioritize? (Choose one).*

peaceful   present   productive

Get Going: *A realistic to do list: may include anything from appointments to surviving the day.*

Must do	**Nice to do**	**Get to do**
important	want	gratitude

Get Real:

Get as honest as possible about what you are feeling, what you need, what capacity you have to give and what makes the most sense for your family today. How can you use awareness to adjust your expectations to your current lived reality? How are you going to be a good mom without striving for perfection? You've got this!

_____

_____

_____

Get Reflective :

I am proud of myself for: _____

_____

_____

even though: _____

_____

Get Some Grace:

I am feeling guilty for: _____

_____

*and so
I need to:*
(Choose one)

   Give myself grace and try again tomorrow

   Give myself grace and apologize

   Give myself grace and seek out tools to improve

   I don't need grace, this guilt is not necessary or productive

Get Positive:

*You did it! What did you get done today? This is your "tada" list.
Fed the kids? Made an appointment? The possibilities are endless.*

Something you accomplished: _____

A mental win: _____

Get Reminiscent:

It's so easy to end our day thinking about what we didn't do or how we messed up. It's easy to forget the special little moments that made us laugh or felt meaningful, too. What's a small thing that you'd like to remember from today?

_____

_____

_____

I can't do it all everyday, but everyday I do something that matters. I'm not defined by what I do but rather who I am. I am a human who loves her kids and I deserve as much grace as anyone else. I deserve to be cared for, too. I am a good mom, and I know this because *I am here, I am aware* and *I am trying.*

Date: _____

Get Affirmed:

I'm a good mom because I love my kid(s) and I am aware enough to know I can't do it all. Every family, every struggle and every season of my motherhood is different and so I won't let one day define what kind of mom I am. My expectations should change with my reality. *I am trying and that matters.*

Get Aware: *Because our unique situation impacts our capacity and knowing this can change our whole day.*

A reality that could make today easier: _____

_____

A reality that could make today harder: _____

_____

Get Your Priorities Straight *You can't be everything all day everyday. Today, what are you going to prioritize? (Choose one).*

peaceful   present   productive

Get Going: *A realistic to do list: may include anything from appointments to surviving the day.*

Must do	Nice to do	Get to do
important	want	gratitude
_____	_____	_____
_____	_____	_____
_____	_____	_____

Get Real:

Get as honest as possible about what you are feeling, what you need, what capacity you have to give and what makes the most sense for your family today. How can you use awareness to adjust your expectations to your current lived reality? How are you going to be a good mom without striving for perfection? You've got this!

_____

_____

_____

Get Reflective :

I am proud of myself for: _____

_____

_____

even though: _____

_____

Get Some Grace:

I am feeling guilty for: _____

_____

and so
I need to:
(Choose one)

- Give myself grace and try again tomorrow
- Give myself grace and apologize
- Give myself grace and seek out tools to improve
- I don't need grace, this guilt is not necessary or productive

Get Positive:
You did it! What did you get done today? This is your "tada" list. Fed the kids? Made an appointment? The possibilities are endless.

Something you accomplished: _____

A mental win: _____

Get Reminiscent:

It's so easy to end our day thinking about what we didn't do or how we messed up. It's easy to forget the special little moments that made us laugh or felt meaningful, too. What's a small thing that you'd like to remember from today?

_____

_____

_____

I can't do it all everyday, but everyday I do something that matters. I'm not defined by what I do but rather who I am. I am a human who loves her kids and I deserve as much grace as anyone else. I deserve to be cared for, too. I am a good mom, and I know this because *I am here, I am aware* and *I am trying.*

TiME TO REFLECT

This part is *really* important.

It's where you pay attention to the hard work you have put into this week in real life and also in these journal pages. It is the checkpoint that you stop at to look at the state of your sense of self of self-worth, self-awareness, self-acceptance and the state of your expectations.

When you do this, keep in mind it is about **progress** not perfection. It is about getting honest about yourself, your motherhood and your circumstances so that you can see what your capacity truly is. Then use this knowledge to have more grace for yourself, less guilt and eventually, more confidence in the things you intentionally choose to prioritize [which are based on your values & capacity].

Slowly but surely, you'll create more space for you again and that space will allow you to enjoy motherhood more, and struggle less. Let's do it.

—

You Are Worthy
You are a human being with human needs, even if you are a mom. You are worthy of love, of care, of rest, of play, of sleep, of nourishment, of joy and of grace. Being imperfect is a part of being human and acknowledging that you have needs is essential to making changes that help those needs get met.

Do you believe you are worthy of these things?   Yes   No   Sometimes

In what ways have you started to see your perception of yourself change this week?

When have you actively chosen **you** this week? What did you do?
How did it feel?

In what ways would you like to see your mindset towards yourself change more?

—

You Have Awareness
Your circumstances are unique, I hope that this week you have been able to become more aware of them and be radically honest about: what resources and supports you have at your disposal; what roadblocks you are facing when it comes to meeting your own expectations; and what values drive how your prioritize that time, energy and overall capacity that you have at this stage of life.

What parts of your life (finances, support system, partner status, mental health or physical health limitations, child stages/ages abilities, personal capacity and day to day circumstances etc) have you become more aware of this week?

How has this awareness helped you to fight guilt, give yourself grace, utilize some of your support system or change expectations for yourself?

How can you become even more self aware this week? How can you use this awareness to struggle a little less with your day to day reality or the way you feel?

—

You Accept Yourself

You cannot be all the things to all the people all the time. You have certain values, limitations and priorities. With the knowledge that you are worthy and the awareness of your reality, you can begin to accept that you cannot prioritize everything all the time. With the nature of being human and life being busy, your capacity will change and with that you can accept yourself.

What are you learning to accept about the limitations you might have that impact your motherhood journey?

What things do you still struggle to accept that you can't do? Or what things are you struggling to accept that you can't change?

What are you going to do differently this coming week that will help you to be more accepting of what you can't change or are struggling to change?

—

Your Expectations are Changing

You have expectations. We all do. We are told that it's important to change them. But how? And which ones? And for how long? The only way we can find the time to prioritize our own wellness and struggle less in motherhood is by letting some things go–even if it's just for a season or a day! By focusing on your priorities, values, limitations and supports I hope you have been able to realize what things you can lower expectations on or take off the priority list all together.

What was your biggest priority this week, and do you think it was a realistic priority to have?

What expectations were you able to shift based on the self-awareness you have been practicing?

What expectations would you like to see yourself shift even more?

Have you been feeling guilt or shame about changing expectations? How can you work on your self-worth & grace in order to combat the negative feelings that come with letting some things go?

Great job. You are doing the work. You are taking the time from the million other things you have to do and using it to be intentional about your motherhood journey and your experience of it. It is not easy. But it is worth it and I am so proud of you. Here's to another week of Honest Mothering. You've got this.

Get Affirmed:

I'm a good mom because I love my kid(s) and I am aware enough to know I can't do it all. Every family, every struggle and every season of my motherhood is different and so I won't let one day define what kind of mom I am. My expectations should change with my reality. *I am trying and that matters.*

Get Aware:
Because our unique situation impacts our capacity and knowing this can change our whole day.

A reality that could make today easier: _____

_____

A reality that could make today harder: _____

_____

Get Your Priorities Straight
You can't be everything all day everyday. Today, what are you going to prioritize? (Choose one).

peaceful   present   productive

Get Going:
A realistic to do list: may include anything from appointments to surviving the day.

Must do	Nice to do	Get to do
important	want	gratitude

Get Real:

Get as honest as possible about what you are feeling, what you need, what capacity you have to give and what makes the most sense for your family today. How can you use awareness to adjust your expectations to your current lived reality? How are you going to be a good mom without striving for perfection? You've got this!

_____

_____

_____

Get Reflective :

I am proud of myself for: _____

_____

_____

even though: _____

_____

Get Some Grace:

I am feeling guilty for: _____

_____

and so
I need to:
(Choose one)

- [ ] Give myself grace and try again tomorrow
- [ ] Give myself grace and apologize
- [ ] Give myself grace and seek out tools to improve
- [ ] I don't need grace, this guilt is not necessary or productive

Get Positive:

You did it! What did you get done today? This is your "tada" list. Fed the kids? Made an appointment? The possibilities are endless.

Something you accomplished: _____

A mental win: _____

Get Reminiscent:

It's so easy to end our day thinking about what we didn't do or how we messed up. It's easy to forget the special little moments that made us laugh or felt meaningful, too. What's a small thing that you'd like to remember from today?

_____

_____

_____

I can't do it all everyday, but everyday I do something that matters. I'm not defined by what I do but rather who I am. I am a human who loves her kids and I deserve as much grace as anyone else. I deserve to be cared for, too. I am a good mom, and I know this because *I am here, I am aware* and *I am trying.*

Date: _____

Get Affirmed:

I'm a good mom because I love my kid(s) and I am aware enough to know I can't do it all. Every family, every struggle and every season of my motherhood is different and so I won't let one day define what kind of mom I am. My expectations should change with my reality. *I am trying and that matters.*

Get Aware: *Because our unique situation impacts our capacity and knowing this can change our whole day.*

A reality that could make today easier: _____

_____

A reality that could make today harder: _____

_____

Get Your Priorities Straight *You can't be everything all day everyday. Today, what are you going to prioritize? (Choose one).*

peaceful   present   productive

Get Going: *A realistic to do list: may include anything from appointments to surviving the day.*

| **Must do** | **Nice to do** | **Get to do** |
important	want	gratitude

Get Real:

Get as honest as possible about what you are feeling, what you need, what capacity you have to give and what makes the most sense for your family today. How can you use awareness to adjust your expectations to your current lived reality? How are you going to be a good mom without striving for perfection? You've got this!

_____

_____

_____

Get Reflective :

I am proud of myself for:

even though:

Get Some Grace:

I am feeling guilty for:

and so
I need to:
(Choose one)

Give myself grace and try again tomorrow

Give myself grace and apologize

Give myself grace and seek out tools to improve

I don't need grace, this guilt is not necessary or productive

Get Positive:

You did it! What did you get done today? This is your "tada" list.
Fed the kids? Made an appointment? The possibilities are endless.

Something you accomplished:

A mental win:

Get Reminiscent:

It's so easy to end our day thinking about what we didn't do or how we messed up. It's easy to forget the special little moments that made us laugh or felt meaningful, too. What's a small thing that you'd like to remember from today?

I can't do it all everyday, but everyday I do something that matters. I'm not defined by what I do but rather who I am. I am a human who loves her kids and I deserve as much grace as anyone else. I deserve to be cared for, too. I am a good mom, and I know this because *I am here, I am aware* and *I am trying.*

Get Affirmed:

I'm a good mom because I love my kid(s) and I am aware enough to know I can't do it all. Every family, every struggle and every season of my motherhood is different and so I won't let one day define what kind of mom I am. My expectations should change with my reality. *I am trying and that matters.*

Get Aware:
Because our unique situation impacts our capacity and knowing this can change our whole day.

A reality that could make today easier: _____
_____

A reality that could make today harder: _____
_____

Get Your Priorities Straight
You can't be everything all day everyday. Today, what are you going to prioritize? (Choose one).

peaceful   present   productive

Get Going:
A realistic to do list: may include anything from appointments to surviving the day.

Must do	Nice to do	Get to do
important	want	gratitude

Get Real:

Get as honest as possible about what you are feeling, what you need, what capacity you have to give and what makes the most sense for your family today. How can you use awareness to adjust your expectations to your current lived reality? How are you going to be a good mom without striving for perfection? You've got this!

_____
_____
_____

Get Reflective :

I am proud of myself for: _____

_____

_____

even though: _____

_____

Get Some Grace:

I am feeling guilty for: _____

_____

*and so
I need to:*
(Choose one)

Give myself grace and try again tomorrow

Give myself grace and apologize

Give myself grace and seek out tools to improve

I don't need grace, this guilt is not necessary or productive

Get Positive:
*You did it! What did you get done today? This is your "tada" list.
Fed the kids? Made an appointment? The possibilities are endless.*

Something you accomplished: _____

A mental win: _____

Get Reminiscent:

It's so easy to end our day thinking about what we didn't do or how we messed up. It's easy to forget the special little moments that made us laugh or felt meaningful, too. What's a small thing that you'd like to remember from today?

_____

_____

_____

I can't do it all everyday, but everyday I do something that matters. I'm not defined by what I do but rather who I am. I am a human who loves her kids and I deserve as much grace as anyone else. I deserve to be cared for, too. I am a good mom, and I know this because *I am here, I am aware* and *I am trying.*

Date: _____

Get Affirmed:

I'm a good mom because I love my kid(s) and I am aware enough to know I can't do it all. Every family, every struggle and every season of my motherhood is different and so I won't let one day define what kind of mom I am. My expectations should change with my reality. *I am trying and that matters.*

Get Aware:
Because our unique situation impacts our capacity and knowing this can change our whole day.

A reality that could make today easier: _____

_____

A reality that could make today harder: _____

_____

Get Your Priorities Straight
You can't be everything all day everyday. Today, what are you going to prioritize? (Choose one).

peaceful   present   productive

Get Going:
A realistic to do list: may include anything from appointments to surviving the day.

| **Must do** | **Nice to do** | **Get to do** |
important	want	gratitude

Get Real:

Get as honest as possible about what you are feeling, what you need, what capacity you have to give and what makes the most sense for your family today. How can you use awareness to adjust your expectations to your current lived reality? How are you going to be a good mom without striving for perfection? You've got this!

_____

_____

_____

Get Reflective :

I am proud of myself for:

even though:

Get Some Grace:

I am feeling guilty for:

and so
I need to:
(Choose one)

Give myself grace and try again tomorrow

Give myself grace and apologize

Give myself grace and seek out tools to improve

I don't need grace, this guilt is not necessary or productive

Get Positive: *You did it! What did you get done today? This is your "tada" list. Fed the kids? Made an appointment? The possibilities are endless.*

Something you accomplished:

A mental win:

Get Reminiscent:

It's so easy to end our day thinking about what we didn't do or how we messed up. It's easy to forget the special little moments that made us laugh or felt meaningful, too. What's a small thing that you'd like to remember from today?

I can't do it all everyday, but everyday I do something that matters. I'm not defined by what I do but rather who I am. I am a human who loves her kids and I deserve as much grace as anyone else. I deserve to be cared for, too. I am a good mom, and I know this because *I am here, I am aware* and *I am trying.*

Date: _____

Get Affirmed:

I'm a good mom because I love my kid(s) and I am aware enough to know I can't do it all. Every family, every struggle and every season of my motherhood is different and so I won't let one day define what kind of mom I am. My expectations should change with my reality. *I am trying and that matters.*

Get Aware: *Because our unique situation impacts our capacity and knowing this can change our whole day.*

A reality that could make today easier: _____

_____

A reality that could make today harder: _____

_____

Get Your Priorities Straight *You can't be everything all day everyday. Today, what are you going to prioritize? (Choose one).*

peaceful   *present*   *productive*

Get Going: *A realistic to do list: may include anything from appointments to surviving the day.*

Must do	**Nice to do**	**Get to do**
important	want	gratitude
_____	_____	_____
_____	_____	_____
_____	_____	_____

Get Real:

Get as honest as possible about what you are feeling, what you need, what capacity you have to give and what makes the most sense for your family today. How can you use awareness to adjust your expectations to your current lived reality? How are you going to be a good mom without striving for perfection? You've got this!

_____

_____

_____

Get Reflective :

I am proud of myself for: _____

_____

_____

even though: _____

_____

Get Some Grace:

I am feeling guilty for: _____

_____

*and so
I need to:*
(Choose one)

☐ Give myself grace and try again tomorrow

☐ Give myself grace and apologize

☐ Give myself grace and seek out tools to improve

☐ I don't need grace, this guilt is not necessary or productive

Get Positive: *You did it! What did you get done today? This is your "tada" list.
Fed the kids? Made an appointment? The possibilities are endless.*

Something you accomplished: _____

A mental win: _____

Get Reminiscent:

It's so easy to end our day thinking about what we didn't do or how we messed up. It's easy to forget the special little moments that made us laugh or felt meaningful, too. What's a small thing that you'd like to remember from today?

_____

_____

_____

I can't do it all everyday, but everyday I do something that matters. I'm not defined by what I do but rather who I am. I am a human who loves her kids and I deserve as much grace as anyone else. I deserve to be cared for, too. I am a good mom, and I know this because *I am here, I am aware* and *I am trying.*

Get Affirmed:

I'm a good mom because I love my kid(s) and I am aware enough to know I can't do it all. Every family, every struggle and every season of my motherhood is different and so I won't let one day define what kind of mom I am. My expectations should change with my reality. *I am trying and that matters.*

Get Aware: *Because our unique situation impacts our capacity and knowing this can change our whole day.*

A reality that could make today easier: _____

_____

A reality that could make today harder: _____

_____

Get Your Priorities Straight *You can't be everything all day everyday. Today, what are you going to prioritize? (Choose one).*

peaceful   present   productive

Get Going: *A realistic to do list: may include anything from appointments to surviving the day.*

Must do	**Nice to do**	**Get to do**
important	want	gratitude
_____	_____	_____
_____	_____	_____
_____	_____	_____

Get Real:

Get as honest as possible about what you are feeling, what you need, what capacity you have to give and what makes the most sense for your family today. How can you use awareness to adjust your expectations to your current lived reality? How are you going to be a good mom without striving for perfection? You've got this!

_____

_____

_____

Get Reflective :

I am proud of myself for: _____

_____

_____

even though: _____

_____

Get Some Grace:

I am feeling guilty for: _____

_____

*and so
I need to:*
(Choose one)

- Give myself grace and try again tomorrow
- Give myself grace and apologize
- Give myself grace and seek out tools to improve
- I don't need grace, this guilt is not necessary or productive

Get Positive:
*You did it! What did you get done today? This is your "tada" list.
Fed the kids? Made an appointment? The possibilities are endless.*

Something you accomplished: _____

A mental win: _____

Get Reminiscent:

It's so easy to end our day thinking about what we didn't do or how we messed up. It's easy to forget the special little moments that made us laugh or felt meaningful, too. What's a small thing that you'd like to remember from today?

_____

_____

_____

I can't do it all everyday, but everyday I do something that matters. I'm not defined by what I do but rather who I am. I am a human who loves her kids and I deserve as much grace as anyone else. I deserve to be cared for, too. I am a good mom, and I know this because *I am here, I am aware* and *I am trying.*

Date: _____

Get Affirmed:

I'm a good mom because I love my kid(s) and I am aware enough to know I can't do it all. Every family, every struggle and every season of my motherhood is different and so I won't let one day define what kind of mom I am. My expectations should change with my reality. *I am trying and that matters.*

Get Aware: *Because our unique situation impacts our capacity and knowing this can change our whole day.*

A reality that could make today easier: _____

_____

A reality that could make today harder: _____

_____

Get Your Priorities Straight   *You can't be everything all day everyday. Today, what are you going to prioritize? (Choose one).*

peaceful   present   productive

Get Going: *A realistic to do list: may include anything from appointments to surviving the day.*

Must do	Nice to do	Get to do
important	want	gratitude
_____	_____	_____
_____	_____	_____
_____	_____	_____

Get Real:

Get as honest as possible about what you are feeling, what you need, what capacity you have to give and what makes the most sense for your family today. How can you use awareness to adjust your expectations to your current lived reality? How are you going to be a good mom without striving for perfection? You've got this!

_____

_____

_____

Get Reflective :

I am proud of myself for: _____

_____

_____

even though: _____

_____

Get Some Grace:

I am feeling guilty for: _____

_____

and so
I need to:
(Choose one)

Give myself grace and try again tomorrow

Give myself grace and apologize

Give myself grace and seek out tools to improve

I don't need grace, this guilt is not necessary or productive

Get Positive: *You did it! What did you get done today? This is your "tada" list. Fed the kids? Made an appointment? The possibilities are endless.*

Something you accomplished: _____

A mental win: _____

Get Reminiscent:

It's so easy to end our day thinking about what we didn't do or how we messed up. It's easy to forget the special little moments that made us laugh or felt meaningful, too. What's a small thing that you'd like to remember from today?

_____

_____

_____

I can't do it all everyday, but everyday I do something that matters. I'm not defined by what I do but rather who I am. I am a human who loves her kids and I deserve as much grace as anyone else. I deserve to be cared for, too. I am a good mom, and I know this because *I am here, I am aware* and *I am trying.*

Get Affirmed:

I'm a good mom because I love my kid(s) and I am aware enough to know I can't do it all. Every family, every struggle and every season of my motherhood is different and so I won't let one day define what kind of mom I am. My expectations should change with my reality. *I am trying and that matters.*

Get Aware:

Because our unique situation impacts our capacity and knowing this can change our whole day.

A reality that could make today easier: _____

_____

A reality that could make today harder: _____

_____

Get Your Priorities Straight

You can't be everything all day everyday. Today, what are you going to prioritize? (Choose one).

peaceful   present   productive

Get Going:

A realistic to do list: may include anything from appointments to surviving the day.

Must do	**Nice to do**	**Get to do**
important	want	gratitude

Get Real:

Get as honest as possible about what you are feeling, what you need, what capacity you have to give and what makes the most sense for your family today. How can you use awareness to adjust your expectations to your current lived reality? How are you going to be a good mom without striving for perfection? You've got this!

_____

_____

_____

Get Reflective :

I am proud of myself for:

even though:

Get Some Grace:

I am feeling guilty for:

and so
I need to:
(Choose one)

- Give myself grace and try again tomorrow
- Give myself grace and apologize
- Give myself grace and seek out tools to improve
- I don't need grace, this guilt is not necessary or productive

Get Positive:

You did it! What did you get done today? This is your "tada" list.
Fed the kids? Made an appointment? The possibilities are endless.

Something you accomplished:

A mental win:

Get Reminiscent:

It's so easy to end our day thinking about what we didn't do or how we messed up. It's easy to forget the special little moments that made us laugh or felt meaningful, too. What's a small thing that you'd like to remember from today?

I can't do it all everyday, but everyday I do something that matters. I'm not defined by what I do but rather who I am. I am a human who loves her kids and I deserve as much grace as anyone else. I deserve to be cared for, too. I am a good mom, and I know this because *I am here, I am aware* and *I am trying.*

Date: _____

Get Affirmed:

I'm a good mom because I love my kid(s) and I am aware enough to know I can't do it all. Every family, every struggle and every season of my motherhood is different and so I won't let one day define what kind of mom I am. My expectations should change with my reality. *I am trying and that matters.*

Get Aware: *Because our unique situation impacts our capacity and knowing this can change our whole day.*

A reality that could make today easier: _____

_____

A reality that could make today harder: _____

_____

Get Your Priorities Straight   *You can't be everything all day everyday. Today, what are you going to prioritize? (Choose one).*

peaceful   present   productive

Get Going: *A realistic to do list: may include anything from appointments to surviving the day.*

Must do	Nice to do	Get to do
important	want	gratitude

Get Real:

Get as honest as possible about what you are feeling, what you need, what capacity you have to give and what makes the most sense for your family today. How can you use awareness to adjust your expectations to your current lived reality? How are you going to be a good mom without striving for perfection? You've got this!

_____

_____

_____

Get Reflective :

I am proud of myself for: _____

_____

_____

even though: _____

_____

Get Some Grace:

I am feeling guilty for: _____

_____

and so
I need to:
(Choose one)

- Give myself grace and try again tomorrow
- Give myself grace and apologize
- Give myself grace and seek out tools to improve
- I don't need grace, this guilt is not necessary or productive

Get Positive:
You did it! What did you get done today? This is your "tada" list.
Fed the kids? Made an appointment? The possibilities are endless.

Something you accomplished: _____

A mental win: _____

Get Reminiscent:

It's so easy to end our day thinking about what we didn't do or how we messed up. It's easy to forget the special little moments that made us laugh or felt meaningful, too. What's a small thing that you'd like to remember from today?

_____

_____

_____

I can't do it all everyday, but everyday I do something that matters. I'm not defined by what I do but rather who I am. I am a human who loves her kids and I deserve as much grace as anyone else. I deserve to be cared for, too. I am a good mom, and I know this because *I am here, I am aware* and *I am trying.*

Date: _____

Get Affirmed:

I'm a good mom because I love my kid(s) and I am aware enough to know I can't do it all. Every family, every struggle and every season of my motherhood is different and so I won't let one day define what kind of mom I am. My expectations should change with my reality. *I am trying and that matters.*

Get Aware: *Because our unique situation impacts our capacity and knowing this can change our whole day.*

A reality that could make today easier: _____

_____

A reality that could make today harder: _____

_____

Get Your Priorities Straight *You can't be everything all day everyday. Today, what are you going to prioritize? (Choose one).*

peaceful   *present*   *productive*

Get Going: *A realistic to do list: may include anything from appointments to surviving the day.*

Must do	Nice to do	Get to do
important	want	gratitude
_____	_____	_____
_____	_____	_____
_____	_____	_____

Get Real:

Get as honest as possible about what you are feeling, what you need, what capacity you have to give and what makes the most sense for your family today. How can you use awareness to adjust your expectations to your current lived reality? How are you going to be a good mom without striving for perfection? You've got this!

_____

_____

_____

Get Reflective :

I am proud of myself for: _____

_____

_____

even though: _____

_____

Get Some Grace:

I am feeling guilty for: _____

_____

*and so
I need to:*
(Choose one)

Give myself grace and try again tomorrow

Give myself grace and apologize

Give myself grace and seek out tools to improve

I don't need grace, this guilt is not necessary or productive

Get Positive: *You did it! What did you get done today? This is your "tada" list. Fed the kids? Made an appointment? The possibilities are endless.*

Something you accomplished: _____

A mental win: _____

Get Reminiscent:

It's so easy to end our day thinking about what we didn't do or how we messed up. It's easy to forget the special little moments that made us laugh or felt meaningful, too. What's a small thing that you'd like to remember from today?

_____

_____

_____

I can't do it all everyday, but everyday I do something that matters. I'm not defined by what I do but rather who I am. I am a human who loves her kids and I deserve as much grace as anyone else. I deserve to be cared for, too. I am a good mom, and I know this because *I am here, I am aware* and *I am trying.*

Get Affirmed:

I'm a good mom because I love my kid(s) and I am aware enough to know I can't do it all. Every family, every struggle and every season of my motherhood is different and so I won't let one day define what kind of mom I am. My expectations should change with my reality. *I am trying and that matters.*

Get Aware: *Because our unique situation impacts our capacity and knowing this can change our whole day.*

A reality that could make today easier: _____

_____

A reality that could make today harder: _____

_____

Get Your Priorities Straight *You can't be everything all day everyday. Today, what are you going to prioritize? (Choose one).*

peaceful   present   productive

Get Going: *A realistic to do list: may include anything from appointments to surviving the day.*

Must do	Nice to do	Get to do
important	want	gratitude

Get Real:

Get as honest as possible about what you are feeling, what you need, what capacity you have to give and what makes the most sense for your family today. How can you use awareness to adjust your expectations to your current lived reality? How are you going to be a good mom without striving for perfection? You've got this!

_____

_____

_____

Get Reflective :

I am proud of myself for: _____

_____

even though: _____

_____

Get Some Grace:

I am feeling guilty for: _____

_____

*and so
I need to:*
(Choose one)

- Give myself grace and try again tomorrow
- Give myself grace and apologize
- Give myself grace and seek out tools to improve
- I don't need grace, this guilt is not necessary or productive

Get Positive:
*You did it! What did you get done today? This is your "tada" list.
Fed the kids? Made an appointment? The possibilities are endless.*

Something you accomplished: _____

A mental win: _____

Get Reminiscent:

It's so easy to end our day thinking about what we didn't do or how we messed up. It's easy to forget the special little moments that made us laugh or felt meaningful, too. What's a small thing that you'd like to remember from today?

_____

_____

_____

I can't do it all everyday, but everyday I do something that matters. I'm not defined by what I do but rather who I am. I am a human who loves her kids and I deserve as much grace as anyone else. I deserve to be cared for, too. I am a good mom, and I know this because *I am here, I am aware* and *I am trying.*

Get Affirmed:

I'm a good mom because I love my kid(s) and I am aware enough to know I can't do it all. Every family, every struggle and every season of my motherhood is different and so I won't let one day define what kind of mom I am. My expectations should change with my reality. *I am trying and that matters.*

Get Aware: *Because our unique situation impacts our capacity and knowing this can change our whole day.*

A reality that could make today easier: _____

_____

A reality that could make today harder: _____

_____

Get Your Priorities Straight *You can't be everything all day everyday. Today, what are you going to prioritize? (Choose one).*

peaceful   present   productive

Get Going: *A realistic to do list: may include anything from appointments to surviving the day.*

Must do important	**Nice to do** want	**Get to do** gratitude
_____	_____	_____
_____	_____	_____
_____	_____	_____

Get Real:

Get as honest as possible about what you are feeling, what you need, what capacity you have to give and what makes the most sense for your family today. How can you use awareness to adjust your expectations to your current lived reality? How are you going to be a good mom without striving for perfection? You've got this!

_____

_____

_____

Get Reflective :

I am proud of myself for: _____

_____

_____

even though: _____

_____

Get Some Grace:

I am feeling guilty for: _____

_____

and so
I need to:
(Choose one)

Give myself grace and try again tomorrow

Give myself grace and apologize

Give myself grace and seek out tools to improve

I don't need grace, this guilt is not necessary or productive

Get Positive:

You did it! What did you get done today? This is your "tada" list.
Fed the kids? Made an appointment? The possibilities are endless.

Something you accomplished: _____

A mental win: _____

Get Reminiscent:

It's so easy to end our day thinking about what we didn't do or how we messed up. It's easy to forget the special little moments that made us laugh or felt meaningful, too. What's a small thing that you'd like to remember from today?

_____

_____

_____

I can't do it all everyday, but everyday I do something that matters. I'm not defined by what I do but rather who I am. I am a human who loves her kids and I deserve as much grace as anyone else. I deserve to be cared for, too. I am a good mom, and I know this because *I am here, I am aware* and *I am trying.*

Date: _____

Get Affirmed:

I'm a good mom because I love my kid(s) and I am aware enough to know I can't do it all. Every family, every struggle and every season of my motherhood is different and so I won't let one day define what kind of mom I am. My expectations should change with my reality. *I am trying and that matters.*

Get Aware: *Because our unique situation impacts our capacity and knowing this can change our whole day.*

A reality that could make today easier: _____

_____

A reality that could make today harder: _____

_____

Get Your Priorities Straight *You can't be everything all day everyday. Today, what are you going to prioritize? (Choose one).*

peaceful   present   productive

Get Going: *A realistic to do list: may include anything from appointments to surviving the day.*

Must do	Nice to do	Get to do
important	want	gratitude

Get Real:

Get as honest as possible about what you are feeling, what you need, what capacity you have to give and what makes the most sense for your family today. How can you use awareness to adjust your expectations to your current lived reality? How are you going to be a good mom without striving for perfection? You've got this!

_____

_____

_____

Get Reflective :

I am proud of myself for:

even though:

Get Some Grace:

I am feeling guilty for:

and so I need to:
(Choose one)

Give myself grace and try again tomorrow

Give myself grace and apologize

Give myself grace and seek out tools to improve

I don't need grace, this guilt is not necessary or productive

Get Positive: *You did it! What did you get done today? This is your "tada" list. Fed the kids? Made an appointment? The possibilities are endless.*

Something you accomplished:

A mental win:

Get Reminiscent:

It's so easy to end our day thinking about what we didn't do or how we messed up. It's easy to forget the special little moments that made us laugh or felt meaningful, too. What's a small thing that you'd like to remember from today?

I can't do it all everyday, but everyday I do something that matters. I'm not defined by what I do but rather who I am. I am a human who loves her kids and I deserve as much grace as anyone else. I deserve to be cared for, too. I am a good mom, and I know this because *I am here, I am aware* and *I am trying.*

Get Affirmed:

I'm a good mom because I love my kid(s) and I am aware enough to know I can't do it all. Every family, every struggle and every season of my motherhood is different and so I won't let one day define what kind of mom I am. My expectations should change with my reality. *I am trying and that matters.*

Get Aware: *Because our unique situation impacts our capacity and knowing this can change our whole day.*

A reality that could make today easier: _____

_____

A reality that could make today harder: _____

_____

Get Your Priorities Straight *You can't be everything all day everyday. Today, what are you going to prioritize? (Choose one).*

peaceful   present   productive

Get Going: *A realistic to do list: may include anything from appointments to surviving the day.*

Must do	Nice to do	Get to do
important	want	gratitude
_____	_____	_____
_____	_____	_____
_____	_____	_____

Get Real:

Get as honest as possible about what you are feeling, what you need, what capacity you have to give and what makes the most sense for your family today. How can you use awareness to adjust your expectations to your current lived reality? How are you going to be a good mom without striving for perfection? You've got this!

_____

_____

_____

Get Reflective :

I am proud of myself for: _____

_____

_____

even though: _____

_____

Get Some Grace:

I am feeling guilty for: _____

and so
I need to:
(Choose one)

Give myself grace and try again tomorrow

Give myself grace and apologize

Give myself grace and seek out tools to improve

I don't need grace, this guilt is not necessary or productive

Get Positive: *You did it! What did you get done today? This is your "tada" list.*
Fed the kids? Made an appointment? The possibilities are endless.

Something you accomplished: _____

A mental win: _____

Get Reminiscent:

It's so easy to end our day thinking about what we didn't do or how we messed up. It's easy to forget the special little moments that made us laugh or felt meaningful, too. What's a small thing that you'd like to remember from today?

_____

_____

_____

I can't do it all everyday, but everyday I do something that matters. I'm not defined by what I do but rather who I am. I am a human who loves her kids and I deserve as much grace as anyone else. I deserve to be cared for, too. I am a good mom, and I know this because *I am here, I am aware* and *I am trying.*

TiME To REFLECT

This part is *really* important.

It's where you pay attention to the hard work you have put into this week in real life and also in these journal pages. It is the checkpoint that you stop at to look at the state of your sense of self of self-worth, self-awareness, self-acceptance and the state of your expectations.

When you do this, keep in mind it is about **progress** not perfection. It is about getting honest about yourself, your motherhood and your circumstances so that you can see what your capacity truly is. Then use this knowledge to have more grace for yourself, less guilt and eventually, more confidence in the things you intentionally choose to prioritize [which are based on your values & capacity].

Slowly but surely, you'll create more space for you again and that space will allow you to enjoy motherhood more, and struggle less. Let's do it.

—

You Are Worthy
You are a human being with human needs, even if you are a mom. You are worthy of love, of care, of rest, of play, of sleep, of nourishment, of joy and of grace. Being imperfect is a part of being human and acknowledging that you have needs is essential to making changes that help those needs get met.

Do you believe you are worthy of these things?　▢ Yes　▢ No　▢ Sometimes

In what ways have you started to see your perception of yourself change this week?

When have you actively chosen **you** this week? What did you do? How did it feel?

In what ways would you like to see your mindset towards yourself change more?

—

You Have Awareness
Your circumstances are unique, I hope that this week you have been able to become more aware of them and be radically honest about: what resources and supports you have at your disposal; what roadblocks you are facing when it comes to meeting your own expectations; and what values drive how your prioritize that time, energy and overall capacity that you have at this stage of life.

What parts of your life (finances, support system, partner status, mental health or physical health limitations, child stages/ages abilities, personal capacity and day to day circumstances etc) have you become more aware of this week?

How has this awareness helped you to fight guilt, give yourself grace, utilize some of your support system or change expectations for yourself?

How can you become even more self aware this week? How can you use this awareness to struggle a little less with your day to day reality or the way you feel?

—

You Accept Yourself
You cannot be all the things to all the people all the time. You have certain values, limitations and priorities. With the knowledge that you are worthy and the awareness of your reality, you can begin to accept that you cannot prioritize everything all the time. With the nature of being human and life being busy, your capacity will change and with that you can accept yourself.
What are you learning to accept about the limitations you might have that impact your motherhood journey?

What things do you still struggle to accept that you can't do? Or what things are you struggling to accept that you can't change?

What are you going to do differently this coming week that will help you to be more accepting of what you can't change or are struggling to change?

—

Your Expectations are Changing
You have expectations. We all do. We are told that it's important to change them. But how? And which ones? And for how long? The only way we can find the time to prioritize our own wellness and struggle less in motherhood is by letting some things go – even if it's just for a season or a day! By focusing on your priorities, values, limitations and supports I hope you have been able to realize what things you can lower expectations on or take off the priority list all together.

What was your biggest priority this week, and do you think it was a realistic priority to have?

What expectations were you able to shift based on the self-awareness you have been practicing?

What expectations would you like to see yourself shift even more?

Have you been feeling guilt or shame about changing expectations? How can you work on your self-worth & grace in order to combat the negative feelings that come with letting some things go?

Great job. You are doing the work. You are taking the time from the million other things you have to do and using it to be intentional about your motherhood journey and your experience of it. It is not easy. But it is worth it and I am so proud of you. Here's to another week of Honest Mothering. You've got this.

Date: _____

Get Affirmed:

I'm a good mom because I love my kid(s) and I am aware enough to know I can't do it all. Every family, every struggle and every season of my motherhood is different and so I won't let one day define what kind of mom I am. My expectations should change with my reality. *I am trying and that matters.*

Get Aware: *Because our unique situation impacts our capacity and knowing this can change our whole day.*

A reality that could make today easier: _____

_____

A reality that could make today harder: _____

_____

Get Your Priorities Straight *You can't be everything all day everyday. Today, what are you going to prioritize? (Choose one).*

peaceful   present   productive

Get Going: *A realistic to do list: may include anything from appointments to surviving the day.*

Must do	**Nice to do**	**Get to do**
important	want	gratitude
_____	_____	_____
_____	_____	_____
_____	_____	_____

Get Real:

Get as honest as possible about what you are feeling, what you need, what capacity you have to give and what makes the most sense for your family today. How can you use awareness to adjust your expectations to your current lived reality? How are you going to be a good mom without striving for perfection? You've got this!

_____

_____

_____

Get Reflective :

I am proud of myself for: _____

_____

_____

even though: _____

_____

Get Some Grace:

I am feeling guilty for: _____

_____

*and so
I need to:*
(Choose one)

- Give myself grace and try again tomorrow
- Give myself grace and apologize
- Give myself grace and seek out tools to improve
- I don't need grace, this guilt is not necessary or productive

Get Positive:

*You did it! What did you get done today? This is your "tada" list.
Fed the kids? Made an appointment? The possibilities are endless.*

Something you accomplished: _____

A mental win: _____

Get Reminiscent:

It's so easy to end our day thinking about what we didn't do or how we messed up. It's easy to forget the special little moments that made us laugh or felt meaningful, too. What's a small thing that you'd like to remember from today?

_____

_____

_____

I can't do it all everyday, but everyday I do something that matters. I'm not defined by what I do but rather who I am. I am a human who loves her kids and I deserve as much grace as anyone else. I deserve to be cared for, too. I am a good mom, and I know this because *I am here, I am aware* and *I am trying.*

Date: _____

Get Affirmed:

I'm a good mom because I love my kid(s) and I am aware enough to know I can't do it all. Every family, every struggle and every season of my motherhood is different and so I won't let one day define what kind of mom I am. My expectations should change with my reality. *I am trying and that matters.*

Get Aware: *Because our unique situation impacts our capacity and knowing this can change our whole day.*

A reality that could make today easier: _____

_____

A reality that could make today harder: _____

_____

Get Your Priorities Straight *You can't be everything all day everyday. Today, what are you going to prioritize? (Choose one).*

peaceful   present   productive

Get Going: *A realistic to do list: may include anything from appointments to surviving the day.*

Must do	Nice to do	Get to do
important	want	gratitude
_____	_____	_____
_____	_____	_____
_____	_____	_____

Get Real:

Get as honest as possible about what you are feeling, what you need, what capacity you have to give and what makes the most sense for your family today. How can you use awareness to adjust your expectations to your current lived reality? How are you going to be a good mom without striving for perfection? You've got this!

_____

_____

_____

Get Reflective :

I am proud of myself for: _____

_____

_____

even though: _____

_____

Get Some Grace:

I am feeling guilty for: _____

_____

and so
I need to:
(Choose one)

Give myself grace and try again tomorrow

Give myself grace and apologize

Give myself grace and seek out tools to improve

I don't need grace, this guilt is not necessary or productive

Get Positive:
You did it! What did you get done today? This is your "tada" list. Fed the kids? Made an appointment? The possibilities are endless.

Something you accomplished: _____

A mental win: _____

Get Reminiscent:

It's so easy to end our day thinking about what we didn't do or how we messed up. It's easy to forget the special little moments that made us laugh or felt meaningful, too. What's a small thing that you'd like to remember from today?

_____

_____

_____

I can't do it all everyday, but everyday I do something that matters. I'm not defined by what I do but rather who I am. I am a human who loves her kids and I deserve as much grace as anyone else. I deserve to be cared for, too. I am a good mom, and I know this because *I am here, I am aware* and *I am trying.*

Date: _____

Get Affirmed:

I'm a good mom because I love my kid(s) and I am aware enough to know I can't do it all. Every family, every struggle and every season of my motherhood is different and so I won't let one day define what kind of mom I am. My expectations should change with my reality. *I am trying and that matters.*

Get Aware: *Because our unique situation impacts our capacity and knowing this can change our whole day.*

A reality that could make today easier: _____

_____

A reality that could make today harder: _____

_____

Get Your Priorities Straight   *You can't be everything all day everyday. Today, what are you going to prioritize? (Choose one).*

peaceful   present   productive

Get Going: *A realistic to do list: may include anything from appointments to surviving the day.*

Must do important	**Nice to do** want	**Get to do** gratitude

Get Real:

Get as honest as possible about what you are feeling, what you need, what capacity you have to give and what makes the most sense for your family today. How can you use awareness to adjust your expectations to your current lived reality? How are you going to be a good mom without striving for perfection? You've got this!

_____

_____

_____

Get Reflective :

I am proud of myself for: _____

_____

_____

even though: _____

_____

Get Some Grace:

I am feeling guilty for: _____

_____

and so
I need to:
(Choose one)

☐ Give myself grace and try again tomorrow

☐ Give myself grace and apologize

☐ Give myself grace and seek out tools to improve

☐ I don't need grace, this guilt is not necessary or productive

Get Positive:

You did it! What did you get done today? This is your "tada" list.
Fed the kids? Made an appointment? The possibilities are endless.

Something you accomplished: _____

A mental win: _____

Get Reminiscent:

It's so easy to end our day thinking about what we didn't do or how we messed up. It's easy to forget the special little moments that made us laugh or felt meaningful, too. What's a small thing that you'd like to remember from today?

_____

_____

_____

I can't do it all everyday, but everyday I do something that matters. I'm not defined by what I do but rather who I am. I am a human who loves her kids and I deserve as much grace as anyone else. I deserve to be cared for, too. I am a good mom, and I know this because *I am here, I am aware* and *I am trying.*

Date: _____

Get Affirmed:

I'm a good mom because I love my kid(s) and I am aware enough to know I can't do it all. Every family, every struggle and every season of my motherhood is different and so I won't let one day define what kind of mom I am. My expectations should change with my reality. *I am trying and that matters.*

Get Aware: *Because our unique situation impacts our capacity and knowing this can change our whole day.*

A reality that could make today easier: _____

_____

A reality that could make today harder: _____

_____

Get Your Priorities Straight   *You can't be everything all day everyday. Today, what are you going to prioritize? (Choose one).*

peaceful   present   productive

Get Going: *A realistic to do list: may include anything from appointments to surviving the day.*

Must do	Nice to do	Get to do
important	want	gratitude
_____	_____	_____
_____	_____	_____
_____	_____	_____

Get Real:

Get as honest as possible about what you are feeling, what you need, what capacity you have to give and what makes the most sense for your family today. How can you use awareness to adjust your expectations to your current lived reality? How are you going to be a good mom without striving for perfection? You've got this!

_____

_____

_____

Get Reflective :

I am proud of myself for: _____
_____
_____

even though: _____
_____

Get Some Grace:

I am feeling guilty for: _____
_____

and so
I need to:
(Choose one)

- Give myself grace and try again tomorrow
- Give myself grace and apologize
- Give myself grace and seek out tools to improve
- I don't need grace, this guilt is not necessary or productive

Get Positive:
You did it! What did you get done today? This is your "tada" list. Fed the kids? Made an appointment? The possibilities are endless.

Something you accomplished: _____

A mental win: _____

Get Reminiscent:

It's so easy to end our day thinking about what we didn't do or how we messed up. It's easy to forget the special little moments that made us laugh or felt meaningful, too. What's a small thing that you'd like to remember from today?

_____
_____
_____

I can't do it all everyday, but everyday I do something that matters. I'm not defined by what I do but rather who I am. I am a human who loves her kids and I deserve as much grace as anyone else. I deserve to be cared for, too. I am a good mom, and I know this because *I am here, I am aware* and *I am trying.*

Date: _____

Get Affirmed:

I'm a good mom because I love my kid(s) and I am aware enough to know I can't do it all. Every family, every struggle and every season of my motherhood is different and so I won't let one day define what kind of mom I am. My expectations should change with my reality. *I am trying and that matters.*

Get Aware: *Because our unique situation impacts our capacity and knowing this can change our whole day.*

A reality that could make today easier: _____

_____

A reality that could make today harder: _____

_____

Get Your Priorities Straight *You can't be everything all day everyday. Today, what are you going to prioritize? (Choose one).*

peaceful   *present*   *productive*

Get Going: *A realistic to do list: may include anything from appointments to surviving the day.*

Must do	**Nice to do**	**Get to do**
important	want	gratitude

Get Real:

Get as honest as possible about what you are feeling, what you need, what capacity you have to give and what makes the most sense for your family today. How can you use awareness to adjust your expectations to your current lived reality? How are you going to be a good mom without striving for perfection? You've got this!

_____

_____

_____

Get Reflective :

I am proud of myself for:

even though:

Get Some Grace:

I am feeling guilty for:

and so
I need to:
(Choose one)

Give myself grace and try again tomorrow

Give myself grace and apologize

Give myself grace and seek out tools to improve

I don't need grace, this guilt is not necessary or productive

Get Positive: *You did it! What did you get done today? This is your "tada" list. Fed the kids? Made an appointment? The possibilities are endless.*

Something you accomplished:

A mental win:

Get Reminiscent:

It's so easy to end our day thinking about what we didn't do or how we messed up. It's easy to forget the special little moments that made us laugh or felt meaningful, too. What's a small thing that you'd like to remember from today?

I can't do it all everyday, but everyday I do something that matters. I'm not defined by what I do but rather who I am. I am a human who loves her kids and I deserve as much grace as anyone else. I deserve to be cared for, too. I am a good mom, and I know this because *I am here, I am aware* and *I am trying.*

Date: _____

Get Affirmed:

I'm a good mom because I love my kid(s) and I am aware enough to know I can't do it all. Every family, every struggle and every season of my motherhood is different and so I won't let one day define what kind of mom I am. My expectations should change with my reality. *I am trying and that matters.*

Get Aware: *Because our unique situation impacts our capacity and knowing this can change our whole day.*

A reality that could make today easier: _____

_____

A reality that could make today harder: _____

_____

Get Your Priorities Straight   *You can't be everything all day everyday. Today, what are you going to prioritize? (Choose one).*

peaceful   present   productive

Get Going: *A realistic to do list: may include anything from appointments to surviving the day.*

Must do	Nice to do	Get to do
important	want	gratitude

Get Real:

Get as honest as possible about what you are feeling, what you need, what capacity you have to give and what makes the most sense for your family today. How can you use awareness to adjust your expectations to your current lived reality? How are you going to be a good mom without striving for perfection? You've got this!

_____

_____

_____

Get Reflective :

I am proud of myself for: _____

_____

_____

even though: _____

_____

Get Some Grace:

I am feeling guilty for: _____

_____

and so
I need to:
(Choose one)

○ Give myself grace and try again tomorrow

○ Give myself grace and apologize

○ Give myself grace and seek out tools to improve

○ I don't need grace, this guilt is not necessary or productive

Get Positive:

You did it! What did you get done today? This is your "tada" list.
Fed the kids? Made an appointment? The possibilities are endless.

Something you accomplished: _____

A mental win: _____

Get Reminiscent:

It's so easy to end our day thinking about what we didn't do or how we messed up. It's easy to forget the special little moments that made us laugh or felt meaningful, too. What's a small thing that you'd like to remember from today?

_____

_____

_____

I can't do it all everyday, but everyday I do something that matters. I'm not defined by what I do but rather who I am. I am a human who loves her kids and I deserve as much grace as anyone else. I deserve to be cared for, too. I am a good mom, and I know this because *I am here, I am aware* and *I am trying.*

Date: _____

Get Affirmed:

I'm a good mom because I love my kid(s) and I am aware enough to know I can't do it all. Every family, every struggle and every season of my motherhood is different and so I won't let one day define what kind of mom I am. My expectations should change with my reality. *I am trying and that matters.*

Get Aware: *Because our unique situation impacts our capacity and knowing this can change our whole day.*

A reality that could make today easier: _____

_____

A reality that could make today harder: _____

_____

Get Your Priorities Straight *You can't be everything all day everyday. Today, what are you going to prioritize? (Choose one).*

peaceful   present   productive

Get Going: *A realistic to do list: may include anything from appointments to surviving the day.*

Must do	**Nice to do**	**Get to do**
important	want	gratitude
_____	_____	_____
_____	_____	_____
_____	_____	_____

Get Real:

Get as honest as possible about what you are feeling, what you need, what capacity you have to give and what makes the most sense for your family today. How can you use awareness to adjust your expectations to your current lived reality? How are you going to be a good mom without striving for perfection? You've got this!

_____

_____

_____

Get Reflective :

I am proud of myself for:

even though:

Get Some Grace:

I am feeling guilty for:

and so
I need to:
(Choose one)

- Give myself grace and try again tomorrow
- Give myself grace and apologize
- Give myself grace and seek out tools to improve
- I don't need grace, this guilt is not necessary or productive

Get Positive:
You did it! What did you get done today? This is your "tada" list.
Fed the kids? Made an appointment? The possibilities are endless.

Something you accomplished:

A mental win:

Get Reminiscent:

It's so easy to end our day thinking about what we didn't do or how we messed up. It's easy to forget the special little moments that made us laugh or felt meaningful, too. What's a small thing that you'd like to remember from today?

I can't do it all everyday, but everyday I do something that matters. I'm not defined by what I do but rather who I am. I am a human who loves her kids and I deserve as much grace as anyone else. I deserve to be cared for, too. I am a good mom, and I know this because *I am here, I am aware* and *I am trying.*

Date: _____

Get Affirmed:

I'm a good mom because I love my kid(s) and I am aware enough to know I can't do it all. Every family, every struggle and every season of my motherhood is different and so I won't let one day define what kind of mom I am. My expectations should change with my reality. *I am trying and that matters.*

Get Aware:
Because our unique situation impacts our capacity and knowing this can change our whole day.

A reality that could make today easier: _____

_____

A reality that could make today harder: _____

_____

Get Your Priorities Straight
You can't be everything all day everyday. Today, what are you going to prioritize? (Choose one).

peaceful   present   productive

Get Going:
A realistic to do list: may include anything from appointments to surviving the day.

Must do	Nice to do	Get to do
important	want	gratitude

Get Real:

Get as honest as possible about what you are feeling, what you need, what capacity you have to give and what makes the most sense for your family today. How can you use awareness to adjust your expectations to your current lived reality? How are you going to be a good mom without striving for perfection? You've got this!

_____

_____

_____

Get Reflective :

I am proud of myself for: _____

_____

_____

even though: _____

_____

Get Some Grace:

I am feeling guilty for: _____

_____

*and so
I need to:*
(Choose one)

- Give myself grace and try again tomorrow
- Give myself grace and apologize
- Give myself grace and seek out tools to improve
- I don't need grace, this guilt is not necessary or productive

Get Positive: *You did it! What did you get done today? This is your "tada" list. Fed the kids? Made an appointment? The possibilities are endless.*

Something you accomplished: _____

A mental win: _____

Get Reminiscent:

It's so easy to end our day thinking about what we didn't do or how we messed up. It's easy to forget the special little moments that made us laugh or felt meaningful, too. What's a small thing that you'd like to remember from today?

_____

_____

I can't do it all everyday, but everyday I do something that matters. I'm not defined by what I do but rather who I am. I am a human who loves her kids and I deserve as much grace as anyone else. I deserve to be cared for, too. I am a good mom, and I know this because *I am here, I am aware* and *I am trying.*

Date: _____

Get Affirmed:

I'm a good mom because I love my kid(s) and I am aware enough to know I can't do it all. Every family, every struggle and every season of my motherhood is different and so I won't let one day define what kind of mom I am. My expectations should change with my reality. *I am trying and that matters.*

Get Aware: *Because our unique situation impacts our capacity and knowing this can change our whole day.*

A reality that could make today easier: _____

_____

A reality that could make today harder: _____

_____

Get Your Priorities Straight *You can't be everything all day everyday. Today, what are you going to prioritize? (Choose one).*

peaceful   *present*   *productive*

Get Going: *A realistic to do list: may include anything from appointments to surviving the day.*

Must do	Nice to do	Get to do
important	want	gratitude

Get Real:

Get as honest as possible about what you are feeling, what you need, what capacity you have to give and what makes the most sense for your family today. How can you use awareness to adjust your expectations to your current lived reality? How are you going to be a good mom without striving for perfection? You've got this!

_____

_____

_____

EVENING

Get Reflective :

I am proud of myself for: _____

_____

_____

even though: _____

_____

Get Some Grace:

I am feeling guilty for: _____

_____

and so I need to:
(Choose one)

- Give myself grace and try again tomorrow
- Give myself grace and apologize
- Give myself grace and seek out tools to improve
- I don't need grace, this guilt is not necessary or productive

Get Positive: *You did it! What did you get done today? This is your "tada" list. Fed the kids? Made an appointment? The possibilities are endless.*

Something you accomplished: _____

A mental win: _____

Get Reminiscent:

It's so easy to end our day thinking about what we didn't do or how we messed up. It's easy to forget the special little moments that made us laugh or felt meaningful, too. What's a small thing that you'd like to remember from today?

_____

_____

_____

I can't do it all everyday, but everyday I do something that matters. I'm not defined by what I do but rather who I am. I am a human who loves her kids and I deserve as much grace as anyone else. I deserve to be cared for, too. I am a good mom, and I know this because *I am here, I am aware* and *I am trying.*

Get Affirmed:

I'm a good mom because I love my kid(s) and I am aware enough to know I can't do it all. Every family, every struggle and every season of my motherhood is different and so I won't let one day define what kind of mom I am. My expectations should change with my reality. *I am trying and that matters.*

Get Aware: *Because our unique situation impacts our capacity and knowing this can change our whole day.*

A reality that could make today easier: _____

_____

A reality that could make today harder: _____

_____

Get Your Priorities Straight   *You can't be everything all day everyday. Today, what are you going to prioritize? (Choose one).*

peaceful   present   productive

Get Going: *A realistic to do list: may include anything from appointments to surviving the day.*

Must do important	Nice to do want	Get to do gratitude

Get Real:

Get as honest as possible about what you are feeling, what you need, what capacity you have to give and what makes the most sense for your family today. How can you use awareness to adjust your expectations to your current lived reality? How are you going to be a good mom without striving for perfection? You've got this!

_____

_____

_____

Get Reflective :

I am proud of myself for: _____

_____

_____

even though: _____

_____

Get Some Grace:

I am feeling guilty for: _____

_____

and so I need to:
(Choose one)

- Give myself grace and try again tomorrow
- Give myself grace and apologize
- Give myself grace and seek out tools to improve
- I don't need grace, this guilt is not necessary or productive

Get Positive:

You did it! What did you get done today? This is your "tada" list. Fed the kids? Made an appointment? The possibilities are endless.

Something you accomplished: _____

A mental win: _____

Get Reminiscent:

It's so easy to end our day thinking about what we didn't do or how we messed up. It's easy to forget the special little moments that made us laugh or felt meaningful, too. What's a small thing that you'd like to remember from today?

_____

_____

_____

I can't do it all everyday, but everyday I do something that matters. I'm not defined by what I do but rather who I am. I am a human who loves her kids and I deserve as much grace as anyone else. I deserve to be cared for, too. I am a good mom, and I know this because *I am here, I am aware* and *I am trying.*

Date: _____

Get Affirmed:

I'm a good mom because I love my kid(s) and I am aware enough to know I can't do it all. Every family, every struggle and every season of my motherhood is different and so I won't let one day define what kind of mom I am. My expectations should change with my reality. *I am trying and that matters.*

Get Aware: *Because our unique situation impacts our capacity and knowing this can change our whole day.*

A reality that could make today easier: _____

_____

A reality that could make today harder: _____

_____

Get Your Priorities Straight   *You can't be everything all day everyday. Today, what are you going to prioritize? (Choose one).*

peaceful   present   productive

Get Going: *A realistic to do list: may include anything from appointments to surviving the day.*

Must do	Nice to do	Get to do
important	want	gratitude

Get Real:

Get as honest as possible about what you are feeling, what you need, what capacity you have to give and what makes the most sense for your family today. How can you use awareness to adjust your expectations to your current lived reality? How are you going to be a good mom without striving for perfection? You've got this!

_____

_____

_____

EVENING

Get Reflective :

I am proud of myself for: _____

_____

_____

even though: _____

_____

Get Some Grace:

I am feeling guilty for: _____

_____

and so
I need to:
(Choose one)

- Give myself grace and try again tomorrow
- Give myself grace and apologize
- Give myself grace and seek out tools to improve
- I don't need grace, this guilt is not necessary or productive

Get Positive:

You did it! What did you get done today? This is your "tada" list. Fed the kids? Made an appointment? The possibilities are endless.

Something you accomplished: _____

A mental win: _____

Get Reminiscent:

It's so easy to end our day thinking about what we didn't do or how we messed up. It's easy to forget the special little moments that made us laugh or felt meaningful, too. What's a small thing that you'd like to remember from today?

_____

_____

_____

I can't do it all everyday, but everyday I do something that matters. I'm not defined by what I do but rather who I am. I am a human who loves her kids and I deserve as much grace as anyone else. I deserve to be cared for, too. I am a good mom, and I know this because *I am here, I am aware* and *I am trying.*

Date: _____

Get Affirmed:

I'm a good mom because I love my kid(s) and I am aware enough to know I can't do it all. Every family, every struggle and every season of my motherhood is different and so I won't let one day define what kind of mom I am. My expectations should change with my reality. *I am trying and that matters.*

Get Aware:
Because our unique situation impacts our capacity and knowing this can change our whole day.

A reality that could make today easier: _____

_____

A reality that could make today harder: _____

_____

Get Your Priorities Straight
You can't be everything all day everyday. Today, what are you going to prioritize? (Choose one).

peaceful   present   productive

Get Going:
A realistic to do list: may include anything from appointments to surviving the day.

Must do	Nice to do	Get to do
important	want	gratitude

Get Real:

Get as honest as possible about what you are feeling, what you need, what capacity you have to give and what makes the most sense for your family today. How can you use awareness to adjust your expectations to your current lived reality? How are you going to be a good mom without striving for perfection? You've got this!

_____

_____

_____

Get Reflective :

I am proud of myself for:

_____

_____

_____

even though:

_____

_____

Get Some Grace:

I am feeling guilty for:

_____

_____

and so
I need to:
(Choose one)

○ Give myself grace and try again tomorrow

○ Give myself grace and apologize

○ Give myself grace and seek out tools to improve

○ I don't need grace, this guilt is not necessary or productive

Get Positive:
You did it! What did you get done today? This is your "tada" list.
Fed the kids? Made an appointment? The possibilities are endless.

Something you accomplished: _____

A mental win: _____

Get Reminiscent:

It's so easy to end our day thinking about what we didn't do or how we messed up. It's easy to forget the special little moments that made us laugh or felt meaningful, too. What's a small thing that you'd like to remember from today?

_____

_____

_____

I can't do it all everyday, but everyday I do something that matters. I'm not defined by what I do but rather who I am. I am a human who loves her kids and I deserve as much grace as anyone else. I deserve to be cared for, too. I am a good mom, and I know this because *I am here, I am aware* and *I am trying.*

Date: _____

Get Affirmed:

I'm a good mom because I love my kid(s) and I am aware enough to know I can't do it all. Every family, every struggle and every season of my motherhood is different and so I won't let one day define what kind of mom I am. My expectations should change with my reality. *I am trying and that matters.*

Get Aware: *Because our unique situation impacts our capacity and knowing this can change our whole day.*

A reality that could make today easier: _____

_____

A reality that could make today harder: _____

_____

Get Your Priorities Straight *You can't be everything all day everyday. Today, what are you going to prioritize? (Choose one).*

peaceful   *present*   *productive*

Get Going: *A realistic to do list: may include anything from appointments to surviving the day.*

Must do important	**Nice to do** want	**Get to do** gratitude
_____	_____	_____
_____	_____	_____
_____	_____	_____

Get Real:

Get as honest as possible about what you are feeling, what you need, what capacity you have to give and what makes the most sense for your family today. How can you use awareness to adjust your expectations to your current lived reality? How are you going to be a good mom without striving for perfection? You've got this!

_____

_____

_____

Get Reflective :

I am proud of myself for: _____

_____

_____

even though: _____

_____

Get Some Grace:

I am feeling guilty for: _____

_____

and so I need to:
(Choose one)

Give myself grace and try again tomorrow

Give myself grace and apologize

Give myself grace and seek out tools to improve

I don't need grace, this guilt is not necessary or productive

Get Positive: *You did it! What did you get done today? This is your "tada" list. Fed the kids? Made an appointment? The possibilities are endless.*

Something you accomplished: _____

A mental win: _____

Get Reminiscent:

It's so easy to end our day thinking about what we didn't do or how we messed up. It's easy to forget the special little moments that made us laugh or felt meaningful, too. What's a small thing that you'd like to remember from today?

_____

_____

_____

I can't do it all everyday, but everyday I do something that matters. I'm not defined by what I do but rather who I am. I am a human who loves her kids and I deserve as much grace as anyone else. I deserve to be cared for, too. I am a good mom, and I know this because *I am here, I am aware* and *I am trying.*

Date: _____

Get Affirmed:

I'm a good mom because I love my kid(s) and I am aware enough to know I can't do it all. Every family, every struggle and every season of my motherhood is different and so I won't let one day define what kind of mom I am. My expectations should change with my reality. *I am trying and that matters.*

Get Aware: *Because our unique situation impacts our capacity and knowing this can change our whole day.*

A reality that could make today easier: _____

_____

A reality that could make today harder: _____

_____

Get Your Priorities Straight *You can't be everything all day everyday. Today, what are you going to prioritize? (Choose one).*

peaceful   present   productive

Get Going: *A realistic to do list: may include anything from appointments to surviving the day.*

Must do important	Nice to do want	Get to do gratitude

Get Real:

Get as honest as possible about what you are feeling, what you need, what capacity you have to give and what makes the most sense for your family today. How can you use awareness to adjust your expectations to your current lived reality? How are you going to be a good mom without striving for perfection? You've got this!

_____

_____

_____

Get Reflective :

I am proud of myself for: _____

_____

_____

even though: _____

_____

Get Some Grace:

I am feeling guilty for: _____

_____

and so
I need to:
(Choose one)

  Give myself grace and try again tomorrow

  Give myself grace and apologize

  Give myself grace and seek out tools to improve

  I don't need grace, this guilt is not necessary or productive

Get Positive:
You did it! What did you get done today? This is your "tada" list.
Fed the kids? Made an appointment? The possibilities are endless.

Something you accomplished: _____

A mental win: _____

Get Reminiscent:

It's so easy to end our day thinking about what we didn't do or how we messed up. It's easy to forget the special little moments that made us laugh or felt meaningful, too. What's a small thing that you'd like to remember from today?

_____

_____

_____

I can't do it all everyday, but everyday I do something that matters. I'm not defined by what I do but rather who I am. I am a human who loves her kids and I deserve as much grace as anyone else. I deserve to be cared for, too. I am a good mom, and I know this because *I am here, I am aware* and *I am trying.*

TiME TO REFLECT

This part is *really* important.

It's where you pay attention to the hard work you have put into this week in real life and also in these journal pages. It is the checkpoint that you stop at to look at the state of your sense of self of self-worth, self-awareness, self-acceptance and the state of your expectations.

When you do this, keep in mind it is about **progress** not perfection. It is about getting honest about yourself, your motherhood and your circumstances so that you can see what your capacity truly is. Then use this knowledge to have more grace for yourself, less guilt and eventually, more confidence in the things you intentionally choose to prioritize [which are based on your values & capacity].

Slowly but surely, you'll create more space for you again and that space will allow you to enjoy motherhood more, and struggle less. Let's do it.

—

You Are Worthy
You are a human being with human needs, even if you are a mom. You are worthy of love, of care, of rest, of play, of sleep, of nourishment, of joy and of grace. Being imperfect is a part of being human and acknowledging that you have needs is essential to making changes that help those needs get met.

Do you believe you are worthy of these things?　　Yes　　No　　Sometimes

In what ways have you started to see your perception of yourself change this week?

When have you actively chosen **you** this week? What did you do? How did it feel?

In what ways would you like to see your mindset towards yourself change more?

—

You Have Awareness
Your circumstances are unique, I hope that this week you have been able to become more aware of them and be radically honest about: what resources and supports you have at your disposal; what roadblocks you are facing when it comes to meeting your own expectations; and what values drive how your prioritize that time, energy and overall capacity that you have at this stage of life.

What parts of your life (finances, support system, partner status, mental health or physical health limitations, child stages/ages abilities, personal capacity and day to day circumstances etc) have you become more aware of this week?

How has this awareness helped you to fight guilt, give yourself grace, utilize some of your support system or change expectations for yourself?

How can you become even more self aware this week? How can you use this awareness to struggle a little less with your day to day reality or the way you feel?

—

You Accept Yourself

You cannot be all the things to all the people all the time. You have certain values, limitations and priorities. With the knowledge that you are worthy and the awareness of your reality, you can begin to accept that you cannot prioritize everything all the time. With the nature of being human and life being busy, your capacity will change and with that you can accept yourself.
What are you learning to accept about the limitations you might have that impact your motherhood journey?

What things do you still struggle to accept that you can't do? Or what things are you struggling to accept that you can't change?

What are you going to do differently this coming week that will help you to be more accepting of what you can't change or are struggling to change?

—

Your Expectations are Changing

You have expectations. We all do. We are told that it's important to change them. But how? And which ones? And for how long? The only way we can find the time to prioritize our own wellness and struggle less in motherhood is by letting some things go–even if it's just for a season or a day! By focusing on your priorities, values, limitations and supports I hope you have been able to realize what things you can lower expectations on or take off the priority list all together.

What was your biggest priority this week, and do you think it was a realistic priority to have?

What expectations were you able to shift based on the self-awareness you have been practicing?

What expectations would you like to see yourself shift even more?

Have you been feeling guilt or shame about changing expectations? How can you work on your self-worth & grace in order to combat the negative feelings that come with letting some things go?

Great job. You are doing the work. You are taking the time from the million other things you have to do and using it to be intentional about your motherhood journey and your experience of it. It is not easy. But it is worth it and I am so proud of you. Here's to another week of Honest Mothering. You've got this.

NOTES

NOTES

NOTES

NOTES

NOTES

NOTES

NOTES

NOTES

NOTES

CONGRATULATIONS MAMA!

You did it!

You made it through to the end of this journal and I want you to know that I am so proud of you.

I hope you will see by now that the load doesn't feel heavy because you are weak, it feels heavy because it is heavy. I hope this journal has helped you let go of the parts of the load that aren't as realistic or valuable to you right now. I hope you are kinder to yourself now too.

Look back on your days, weeks and months and see just how much you have grown.

Think back to the beginning:
How did you feel about yourself? _____

_____

What were you prioritizing? _____

_____

Where were you focusing your time &
energy that was maybe weighing you down? _____

_____

Think about now:
What are you better able to prioritize without feeling guilty? _____

_____

How often are you going to bed feeling
guilty compared to before you started? _____

_____

What positive mindset shifts have you made? _____

_____

How has your internal dialogue shifted? _____

_____

Owning our motherhood, practicing self-awareness and self-compassion and setting realistic expectations are all a continuous journey. This is not a destination but a jumpstart point for you.

I hope you can take the mindset shift, the tools, resources and experiences you have had while doing this guided journal and apply them to your life going forward. Our motherhood journeys are always changing.

Come stay hi on the 'gram and share your wins with me using #HonestMomJournal I can't wait to hear from you.

Libby

P.S. Make sure you flick back through your journal making note of the positives from the end of each day. When you look at them all together, you've got some special memories there!

Libby Ward is a digital creator, speaker, and mental health advocate with a deep commitment to changing the motherhood narrative and breaking cycles of trauma. Every week, Libby's content reaches millions of women around the world and she has grown a dedicated community of over 1.5M on social media in just two years. She has been recognized as a mental health advocate by *TikTok*, and has been featured on *The Tamron Hall Show*, *Global News*, *Motherly*, *Insider* and media outlets around the world.

As a thought leader in today's difficult and complex experiences of mental health, Libby is focused on reaching more women with her perspective changing stories . Find her at **@diaryofanhonestmom** on Instagram, Tiktok and on her website diaryofanhonestmom.com and fall in love with her authentic content sure to inspire and entertain you each day.

@diaryofanhonestmom   diaryofanhonestmom.com